TREASURES OF THE ZUNI

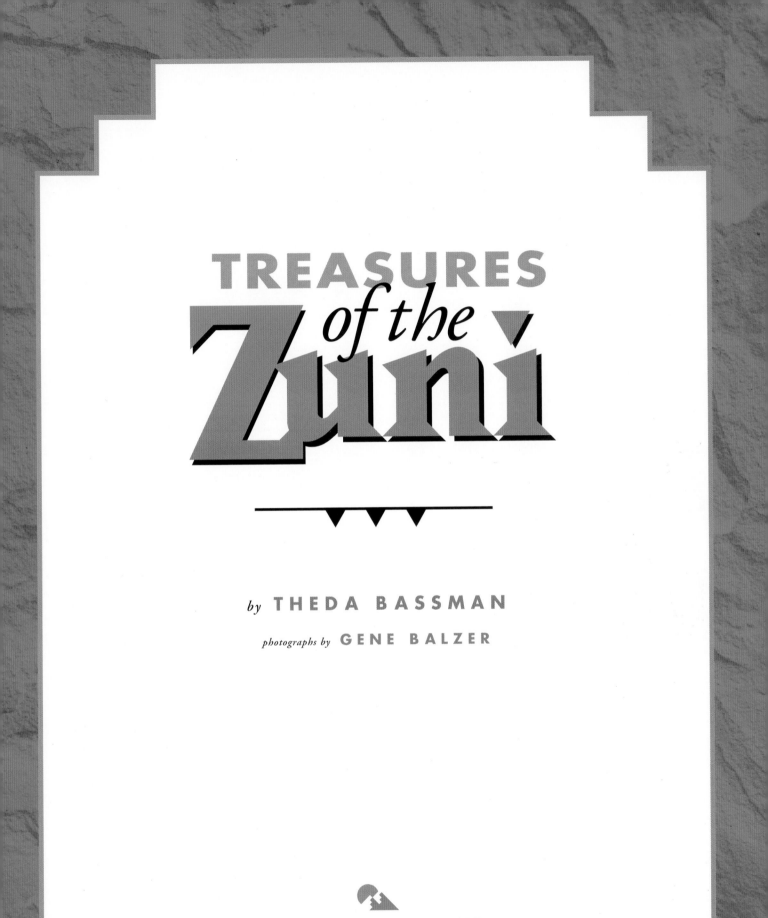

TREASURES *of the* Zuni

by **THEDA BASSMAN**

photographs by **GENE BALZER**

NORTHLAND PUBLISHING

This book is dedicated to Greg Hofmann
to honor a friendship that grew with warmth
and love for over twenty-five years.

The display type was set in Matrix
The text type was set in AGaramond
Designed by Rudy J. Ramos
Edited by Kathleen Bryant and Erin Murphy
Production supervised by Lisa Brownfield
All photographs by Gene Balzer
Manufactured in Hong Kong by
South Sea International Press Ltd.

FIRST IMPRESSION
ISBN 0-87358-674-3

Library of Congress Catalog Card Number 96-36125
Cataloging-in-Publication Data
Bassman, Theda.
    Treasures of the Zuni / by Theda Bassman.
        p.   cm.
    Includes bibliographical references and index.
        ISBN 0–87358–674–3 (pbk.)
    1. Zuni art. 2. Zuni Indians—Material culture. I. Title.
    E99.Z9B337 1997
    704'.03979—dc20   96–36125

0619/7.5M/3-97

OTHER BOOKS BY THEDA BASSMAN

Hopi Kachina Dolls and Their Carvers

The Kachina Dolls of Cecil Calnimptewa Their Power Their Splendor

The Beauty of Hopi Jewelry

Zuni Jewelry, which was co-authored with Michael Bassman

*Treasures of the Hopi

*Treasures of the Navajo

The Beauty of Navajo Jewelry

*Also available from Northland Publishing

Artwork dimensions in photo captions refer to height or length
unless otherwise specified.
When two dimensions are given, they refer to height x width.

Frontispiece: Lone Mountain turquoise bracelet, earrings, and rings,
by Edith Tsabetsaye. The bracelet has 196 stones; the earrings, 109
stones; the oval ring, 65 stones; and the round ring, 61 stones. This set
won First Prize at the Gallup Inter-Tribal Indian Ceremonial in Gallup,
New Mexico, in 1993. *Courtesy of the artist*

Page vi: Pot with sun face, dragonflies, and Long-haired Kachinas,
17 in. high, by Randy Nahohai.

Clay sculpture of the Corn Maiden or Elashdoke, 10 in. high, by Randy
Nahohai. The Corn Maiden represents the Child-Bearing Mother and is
given to a woman who has not been able to become pregnant. This gift
will insure fertility.

Bronze sculpture of the Corn Maiden, by Randy Nahohai. This is the
only limited edition bronze sculpture that has been made in the village
of Zuni. *Courtesy of Turquoise Village*

Page viii: Rainbow Spirits, acrylic, 15 in. x 30 in., by Duane Dishta.
This painting depicts two Rainbow Dancers, Ahmetolela-ot'tsi (Wright,
page 127), and three Downy Feathers Hanging Kachinas, Upikaiapona
(Wright, page 87). *Courtesy of Turquoise Village*

Belt buckle and bola tie set inlaid with white mother-of-pearl, coral,
turquoise, jet, and gold lip mother-of-pearl, by Carol and Wilton Niiha.
Courtesy of Running Bear Zuni Trading Post

Two pots with lizards, by Noreen Simplicio. *Courtesy of Turquoise Village*

Pottery sculpture of Shalako Kachina, the Courier of the Gods (Wright,
page 36), by Randy Nahohai. This won second prize at the Zuni Show
of the Museum of Northern Arizona in Flagstaff in 1993. *Private collection*

Round needlepoint pin with Sleeping Beauty turquoise, by Floyd Etsate.
Courtesy of Turquoise Village

Needlepoint pin with Sleeping Beauty turquoise and silver dangles,
by Irma and Octavius Seowtewa. *Courtesy of Turquoise Village*

Bear fetish made of serpentine with shell arrowhead, by Anderson
Weahkee. *Private collection*

Three-strand fetish necklace strung on olivella shell heishe, by Dinah and
Pete Gasper. Necklace has ninety-nine fetishes consisting of owls, fish,
rams, mountain lions, ducks, turtles, frogs, birds, tadpoles, foxes, beavers,
and bears. Stones and shells used are green snail shell, dolomite, pink coral,
spiny oyster shell, turquoise, coral, amber, sugilite, lapis lazuli, malachite,
gold lip mother-of-pearl, jet, spotted serpentine, and pink shell.
Courtesy of Roxanne and Greg Hofmann

Cover and back cover: All photos are pictured in the text except orange
alabaster fetish bear with village scene, 20 in. x 15 in., by Eddington
Hannaweeke. *Private collection*

CONTENTS

▼▼▼

ACKNOWLEDGMENTS

▼ ▼ ▼

My thanks to the following people who so graciously permitted their crafts to be photographed:

Barbara and Chuck Cooper
Ola and Tony Eriacho
Dr. T. R. Frisbie
Roxanne and Greg Hofmann
Beverly Vander Wagen Hurlbut
Judy Johnsen
Martin Link
Al Myman
Milford Nahohai
Malcolm Maxwell Newman
Dan Ostermiller
Ralph Singleton
Frances Snyder
Edith Tsabetsaye
And all of the private collectors who wish to remain anonymous

Additional thanks to the trading posts and their employees, who were always ready not only to provide me with crafts but also to answer my numerous questions:

Sangelita Dishta
Greg Hofmann
Mikki Lewis
Milford Nahohai
Pueblo of Zuni Arts & Crafts
Running Bear Zuni Trading Post
Kit South
Jay Soseeah
Turquoise Village

As always, my gratitude to my husband, Michael, who is constantly ready to help, putting aside his own interests. I could not have written this book without his assistance and support.

Lastly, my thanks to my photographer, Gene Balzer, whose artistry makes the book come alive.

Introduction

THE PUEBLO OF Zuni is located in New Mexico about forty miles south of Gallup and is the largest pueblo in New Mexico. The Pueblo has a present day population of 9,641 residents, consisting of 8,933 Zunis, or *A:shiwi* as they call themselves; 256 people of other Indian tribal origin; and 465 non-Indians. They live on lands that encompass 409,344 acres. They have their own school system, courts, and tribal government. English is the language of the school and the marketplace. The Zuni language is quite distinctive, and it is totally unrelated to the language of any other tribe of the Southwest. The community has preserved its own language which nearly all Zunis speak, especially when they interact with each other at home.

Most of the people live at an elevation between six thousand and seven thousand feet, where annual rainfall is between eleven and sixteen inches. Zuni has beautiful red sandstone cliffs that serve as a spectacular backdrop. *Dowa Yalanne*, Corn Mountain, is the sacred mountain of Zuni. There are also rich grazing lands, dotted with piñon and juniper trees.

The Zunis have maintained a matriarchal society as the base of kinship. The husband lives with his wife and mother-in-law in the traditional way. It is the close-knit groups and the elaborate religious ceremonies that bind and hold the Zuni community together.

From 1540 to 1740 the Zunis occupied seven villages in the province of Shiwona: *Hawikuh* (meaning To Tie The Wild Grasses), *Halona* (Ant Hill), *Matsaki* or *Matsayka* (Salt City), *Kiakime* (Eagle), *Kechibawe* (White Wash Village), *Binawa* (Windy Place). The name of the seventh village is unknown. The present Pueblo is built on the old site of Halona.

In 1539 a Franciscan monk named Fray Marcos de Niza set out from Mexico to determine if Shiwona could be the fabled Seven Cities of Cibola settlement, which supposedly held gold treasures. His advance scouting party was led by Estaban, a Moorish slave who had explored the Gulf of Mexico and Texas with Cabeza de Vaca. Estaban had had earlier successes in dealing with Indian tribes, but this was not to be in Zuni. The Zunis found him arrogant, obnoxious, and insulting to the women, and "cured his bad manners" by killing him after he reached Hawikuh. De Niza received news of Esteban's death, but he traveled only far enough to catch a small glimpse of Hawikuh. He went back to Mexico, where he deliberately lied that he had found the Kingdom of Cibola with its gold treasures.

The following year Francisco Coronado led an expedition that was guided by Fray de Niza. The trip was so arduous that by the time Coronado reached Hawikuh, he was more interested in food for his soldiers than gold. The farmers of Zuni did not even know what gold was. Coronado's frustration led to anger, and the anger led to the massacre of the village. Then Coronado left.

Forty years later the Spanish returned, and clashes resulted. The various pueblos were at a hopeless disadvantage. The Spanish horsemen were armed with steel weapons; the process of subjugation began. The colonizers used the Indians as slave labor.

In 1642 and again in 1680, the various pueblos in Arizona and New Mexico joined forces and revolted. In 1680 the Pueblo Indians revolted against the Spanish despite the distance between villages, the language barrier, and the Pueblo tradition of each village tending to its own affairs. The pain and humiliation suffered by the Pueblo Indians erupted into anger. Popé, a medicine man from the Pueblo of San Juan, channeled this anger and organized a revolt by all the villages from Taos to the Hopi mesas. The unity the Indians achieved broke the back of the Spanish colonization in the Southwest. The Spanish abandoned their last stronghold in Santa Fe, leaving some four hundred dead in the entire region.

However, twelve years later Don Diego de Vargas reconquered the Indians and established Spanish rule over the Southwest. The three-headed juggernaut of Spanish civilization—priests, presidios, and patronés—systematically and ponderously disrupted and almost destroyed the Indians. Interestingly enough, the Hopis, normally the most peaceful of the Pueblos, were never reconquered. Their resolve to fight back and remain free prevailed.

After the reconquest of 1692, the Zunis resettled in the valley of the Zuni River, but only in one village, Halona. In spite of the Spanish intrusion, the Zunis retained much of their traditional culture and religion. Even though the Spanish introduced some beneficial changes (such as burros, horses, sheep, and wheat), they were instrumental in bringing in a wide variety of destructive new diseases that caused a drastic reduction in the Zuni population.

Since the Pueblo Indians were in contact with Spanish colonizers for some four hundred years, they adopted some Spanish elements into their culture. For example, all pueblo villages have a Catholic church. Although some Zunis are Catholic, they maintain their own prior religion as well, in spite of the differences.

The old Zuni Mission, now called Nuestra Señora de Guadalupe de Zuni, was built in 1629 and completed in 1932 by the Zunis under the supervision of Franciscan friars. It is one of the oldest missions in the United States. In 1821 the friars withdrew from Zuni to return to Mexico, which had achieved independence from Spain. The old Mission fell into ruin, and over the years it decayed from weather and neglect. In 1966, Franciscan Friar Niles

Kraft, the Zuni Tribe, the Bureau of Indian Affairs, and the National Park Service jointly began the restoration of the old Mission, which continued until late 1969. The Mission is now actively used.

After the rebuilding of the church was finished, a renowned Zuni artist, Alex Seowtewa, began a project to paint a series of life-size Kachinas, or *Kokkos,* as the Zunis call them, on the walls of the nave of the Mission. Alex is assisted by his sons, Kenneth and Edwin. The mural project will probably be completed by the year 2000, depending upon future funding from the Zuni tribe, the Catholic Church, the National Endowment for the Arts, and contributions from the private sector. The state of New Mexico is also helping finance the project via a grant. Alex has received many prestigious art awards, not only in New Mexico but also in the Soviet Union, for his work on the Mission.

In addition to the old Mission, there is St. Anthony's Catholic Church, established in 1922.

Religion is the center of all life in this tribe. As expected in an agricultural society, rain is the center of many religious observances. Ceremonies are held to control the weather so that crops may grow and mature as a result of the Zuni rituals.

According to the Zuni religion, Kóthluwalawan represents the dwellings and lake inside the mountains called Kóthluwalanne. This is the Zuni Heaven and is the place where all Zunis go after death. This is also where the Zuni River flows between two mountains and then joins with the Little Colorado River.

Every four years, between forty and sixty Zunis set out on a strenuous religious pilgrimage that covers more than 110 miles in four days. The Zunis who make this ceremonial journey represent all the tribal members. They make offerings, say prayers, gather sacred paint pigments, and eventually reach Kóthluwalanne, where their activities are directed at bringing peace, order, and prosperity, not only to Zunis, but to the entire world.

On August 28, 1984, the Congress of the United States passed Senate Bill 2201, "To Convey Certain Lands to the Zuni Tribe for Religious Purposes." This enabled the Zunis to include almost twelve thousand acres of land encompassing the area of Kóthluwalanne as part of their land. This bill protected the Zunis' right to make their traditional journey to their sacred area without disturbance or desecration of the sacred site. Difficulties had arisen regarding the pathway to Kóthluwalanne, and the tribe, through its attorneys, was able to convince the United States government to protect the rights of the Tribe against a landowner who wanted to interfere with the traditional sojourn. The litigation ended with a judgment in favor of the Zuni Tribe, and it was awarded the new reservation land in Arizona. Now its members could travel along the "established pathway" without interference.

Only the religious leaders, such as

the kiva leaders and the men representing certain Kachinas (the Shalakos, Mud Head Clowns, Longhorns, and Fire Gods), are permitted to make the special trip every four years. It is believed that the spirits of the Zunis who have died make the journey to Kóthluwalanne. The leaders go there as emissaries to bring the spirits of their ancestors back to the village, and to pray and ask for prosperity and blessings for the people as well as for the village as a whole.

There are six Shalako Kachinas, representing each of the Pueblo's kiva groups.

Each Shalako is sent to a specific home in the community for an all-night house blessing and dance. The Shalako dances are held each year in late November or early December. Other Kachina dances take place in the spring and summer months.

The Zuni reservation does not have the vast mineral deposits of the Navajo lands. Even though there is sufficient water to irrigate crops and support limited livestock, the main economic activity at Zuni is arts and crafts, with jewelry being the most widely known. The greatest natural resource of Zuni is the artistic creativity of its people.

It is estimated that 50 to 75 percent of Zuni family income springs from arts and crafts. Because most of the artwork emanates from the home, the income makes it possible for people to stay in Zuni with their families. The arts nourish the community in a material sense. Producing Zuni crafts involves working at home, sometimes individually, but most often with other family members. Arts and crafts at Zuni is a cottage industry, and each cottage (household) specializes in the production of certain kinds of work—jewelry, fetishes, pottery, paintings, Kachina dolls, and beadwork. In general, certain designs will "belong" to a particular family, and these designs will be passed from older family members to younger ones. There is probably no village in North America with a higher concentration of skilled craftspeople than the Pueblo of Zuni.

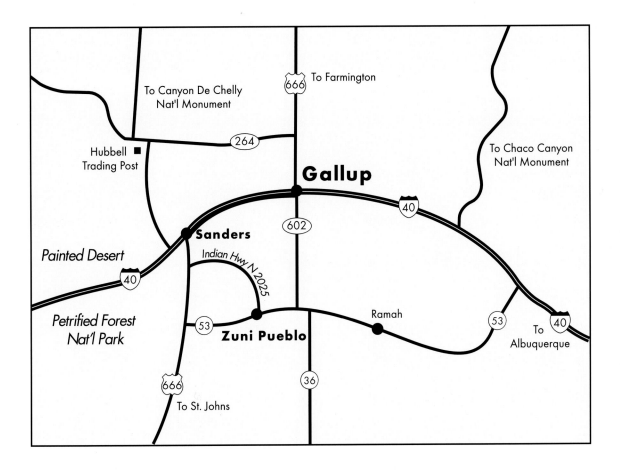

ALL WOOD-CARVED, *left to right:*

Whobone Shelowa, the Santo Domingo Kokoshi (Wright, page 87) with Clemhoktoni (Wright, page 111).

Saiyatasha, the Rain Priest of the North (Wright, page 32).

Shalako, the Courier of the Gods (Wright, page 36) with three Koyemshis: Kalutsi, the Infant or Suwitsana (Wright, page 41), Posuki, the Pouter (Wright, page 41), and Tsathlashi, the Old Youth (Wright, page 41).

Shulawitsi, the Little Pekwin or Little Fire God (Wright, page 32) with cloud, rain, and village designs.

Kianakwe Shelow'ona, Red Kianakwe of the South (Wright, page 76) with Koyemshi Awan Pekwin, the Speaker of the Sun (Wright, page 40).

All made by Tiffany Tsabetsaye.

Courtesy of Turquoise Village

Kachinas

A KACHINA IS a supernatural being. The men of Zuni depict these beings in costumes, masks, and paints. A Kachina is also represented in the form of carved wooden dolls made from the root of the cottonwood tree. Kachina dolls are presented by Kachina dancers to Zuni children during ceremonial activities in order to help the children learn the importance and significance of the specific Kachina spirit.

As supernatural beings, the Kachinas visit the village in the form of costumed dancers to bring rain for the crops and to foster prosperity. The costumed dancers wear masks made of leather, painted with symbolic representations of the spirits, such as birds or animals. The masks also symbolize the sun, rain, clouds, and other elements of nature. Masks convert the wearers into supernatural beings. The mask is not only a sacred object, but also a work of art. It is adorned with feathers, hair, yarn, fur, ribbons, and paints. Feathers are conspicuous as ornaments, and usually the importance of the Kachina can be seen by the variety and quantity of the feathers. All Kachinas use the downy feather from the breast of the eagle. The downy feather is considered the breath of rain. Some Kachinas who wear no other feathers have downy feathers in their ears. Other Kachinas wear eagle tail feathers, owl feathers, turkey tail and breast feathers, and yellow macaw breast feathers.

The Zuni male spends much of his life in ceremonial participation. When a boy becomes eight years old he is initiated into a specific society. He becomes involved in religious activities, including prayers, songs, and dances. Ceremonies are extremely important in Zuni life because they help control the weather and aid the crops in growing productively.

The Kachinas perform two types of rituals. One is held in the sacred ceremonial chambers, called the kiva. The rite is closed to the public. The other is usually performed in the plaza and is usually open to the public.

All adult males belong to the Kachina Society, which presents the masked dances. Membership in the Society is treasured by the Zuni. There are six kivas in the Pueblo, and each kiva presents at least three group dances during the year. Summer solstice ceremonies revolve around rain, prayers, and retreats. Winter solstice ceremonies are mainly concerned with fertility rites. The final series of dances, held after the Shalako ceremony, is a "signature" of each kiva, a traditional performance before the Kachinas go home. The dates of the dances are not fixed, but they are usually held when the Kiva Chief feels that the dancers are sufficiently prepared to perform the songs, chants, and dances.

The six kivas in the Zuni Pueblo are Hekiapawa Kiva, Heiwa Kiva, Uptsanna Kiva, Muhewa Kiva, Chuppawa Kiva, and Ohewa Kiva. The kiva itself is rectangular in shape and is on the ground level. After a performance is over, the dancers go to a nearby building, climb up a ladder on the outside of a doorless room, and then down a ladder that sticks out of this room or chamber—the kiva. The special features of the kiva interior are an altar, a fireplace, and built-in benches for the men who have come for ceremonial performances.

The kivas present extra dances after the required dances during the winter or summer solstice. The dances are varied and not as struc-

tured as those that require Society assistance, long prayers, and prayer sticks. In these dances the young men perform with inventiveness and creativity, using flashy costumes and unusual footwork. The dances usually reflect the needs of the village. For example, a Cow Dance is performed to ensure an increase in cattle, a Corn Dance, to ensure the growth of corn.

The Zuni Kachina dolls are different from the Kachina dolls of the Hopi. They are not "action" dolls and are almost always in a staid position. Most of the dolls are not all wood-carved and are beautifully dressed in cloth, yarn, feathers, and fur. There are Zuni carvers, such as Felino Eriacho and Tiffany Tsabetsaye, who have been making all wood-carved dolls, and who are doing an excellent job. When purchasing a doll, it is important to look for proper proportion in the body, hands, and feet, although this is difficult to do with cloth and feathered dolls. The collector's barometer should be how pleasing the Kachina doll is to the eye.

NOTE: *Unless otherwise specified, Kachina dolls are referenced to Barton Wright's* Kachinas of the Zuni, *published in 1985 by Northland Press, Flagstaff, Arizona.*

THE FOLLOWING ARE EXPLANATIONS OF THE PURPOSE AND FUNCTION OF THE KACHINAS SHOWN IN THE PHOTOGRAPHS.

A:chi'ya'ladaba, the Knifewing Dancer, is not a Kachina but is a mystic figure and has been a symbol of protection for the Zuni people for centuries. This figure is a symbol of wisdom, strength, courage, and honor.

Ahmetolela-ot'tsi, the Rainbow Dancer, is a quasi-religious figure.

Anahoho whips the boys who are being initiated.

Atoshle frightens the children so they will behave.

Clemhoktoni is a dance leader in the Hilili Dance.

Hehe'a, the Blunderer, is a helper to the Oky'enawe and carries all the material necessary for the grinding of the corn. He is also very clumsy.

Hemokatsiki or *Ahe'a* is the grandmother of all the Kachinas.

Hilili Kohanna, the Corn Hilili, takes the corn to the Hilili Okya and carries it to the ceremonial house.

Hututu, Saiyatasha's Deputy or Pekwin, reinforces all that the Saiyatasha does.

The *Kianakwes* are not Kachinas, but during their dance they distribute food and commodities to the Zuni.

Kokokshi, the Good or Beautiful Kachina, is a rainmaker.

Kokwele or *Oky'enawe* brings seeds to the houses for planting.

Kolowisi, the Water Serpent, brings corn and seeds to the young boys.

The *Koyemshi* are called the Mud Head Clowns and are very wise but foolish and funny. They satirize Zuni officials and the relationships between women and men, and make fun of their in-laws. They are called the fathers of the Zuni and play an important part in Zuni life.

Kumanshi, Comanche Dance, is an unmasked dance and a partly religious one.

Kumanshi Domda Caynona is the drummer for the Kumanshi Dance.

Laguna Chakwaina, also called **Drum Chakwaina, Chahumoawe,** or **Chamokawistowe,** dances in a dance that was borrowed from the Laguna people.

Nahalisho is a Corn Dancer and has clouds painted on his face so that rain will come and the corn will grow.

Nahalilsh'Okya, the Corn Dance Girl, accompanies the Nahalisho.

Pasikiapa Mosona, the Wide Sleeves Leader, has a strong resemblance to the Hopi Kachina called the Velvet Shirt.

Pasikiapa Tese Akenona Okya, the Wide Sleeves Pottery Drum Girl, is the drummer for the Pasikiapa Dance.

Rainbow Spirits, non-Kachinas, symbolize beauty.

Saiyatasha or Long Horn brings long life to the Zuni people and arranges the Shalako Ceremony.

Saiyathlia Puhu-atinakwe chases away all of the bad things that have happened in the past year.

Salimopia Kachinas are runners and also guards to the highest of the Kachinas and to the ceremonies.

Shalako is the Courier of the Gods and brings corn, seeds, and fruit to the Zuni.

Shalako Anuthlona is also called the Shalako Warrior and is the alternate for the Shalako. He helps the Shalako with the heavy mask.

Shulawitsi Kachinas are the Little Pekwin or Little Fire Gods, and they take care of the sun. They carry a juniper bark torch for the lighting of the prayer sticks. They are also hunters.

Shulawitsi An Tatchu is the Shulawitsi's ceremonial father and helps him light his torch and assists him in the planting of the prayer sticks.

Siwuluhsiwa is the mother of the Koyemshi and takes care of them.

Suyuki captures the naughty children and is said to eat them.

Thlelashoktipona or Wooden Ears is a runner.

Tone-ah represents the turkey.

Upikaiapona, the Downy Feathers Hanging Kachina, is a rainmaker.

Upo'yona is Pautiwa's son and dances in the various dances, as Pautiwa does not dance.

Wakashi, the Cow Kachina, says prayers for the increase of the cows.

Wakashi Awan Peyenokwe starts the song in the Wakashi Dance.

Whobone Shelowa is the Santo Domingo Kokoshi.

Wilatsukwe Peyenokwee, the Apache Talking Leader, is the leader of the Wilatsukwe Dance.

Yamuhakto is the Wood Carrier, an assistant of Saiyatasha who helps him bring wood to the Zuni.

KACHINA DOLLS FROM YEARS PAST,

left to right:

Salimopia Kohan'ona, the White Warrior of the East (Wright, page 59), 12¾ in. high, made in 1960s, artist unknown. *Courtesy of Beverly Vander Wagen Hurlbut*

Kolowisi *(at front),* the Water Serpent (Wright, page 55), 8 in. long, made in late 1950s by Steven Comosona. *Courtesy of Martin Link*

Kumanshi, Comanche (Wright, page 121), 16 in. high, made in early 1960s by Bernard Comosona. Note the embroidered sash. *Courtesy of Martin Link*

Shalako, the Courier of the Gods (Wright, page 36), 10½ in. high, made in 1960s, artist unknown. This is an unmasked Shalako with moveable arms. *Courtesy of Beverly Vander Wagen Hurlbut*

Shalako, the Courier of the Gods (Wright, page 36), 21 in. high, made in early 1960s by Art Kelestawa. *Courtesy of Martin Link*

Hilili Kohanna, the Corn Hilili (Wright, page 111), 14 in. high, made in early 1960s by Steven Comosona. Note the embroidered sash. *Courtesy of Martin Link*

Three Shalako Kachinas (Wright, page 36), 27 in. high, by Emerson Vallo.

Courtesy of Roxanne and Greg Hofmann

A COLLECTION OF MINIATURE KACHINA DOLLS:

UPPER ROW, *left to right:* Salimopia Thlian'ona, the Blue Warrior of the West (Wright, page 59).

Shulawitsi, the Little Pekwin or Little Fire God (Wright, page 32).

Kianakwe Itapanahnan'ona, Many-colored Kianakwe of the Zenith (Wright, 76).

Shalako, the Courier of the Gods (Wright, page 36).

Salimopia Kohan'ona, the White Warrior of the East (Wright, page 59).

Saiyatasha, the Rain Priest of the North or Long Horn (Wright, page 32).

CENTER ROW, *left to right:* Hututu, Saiyatasha's Deputy or Pekwin (Wright, page 32).

Upo'yona, Pautiwa's son (Wright, page 85).

Yamuhakto, the Wood Carrier (Wright, page 32).

Hehe'a, the Blunderer (Wright, pages 72 and 109).

Salimopia Thluptsin'ona, the Yellow Warrior of the North (Wright, page 59).

LOWER ROW, *left to right:* Kokokshi, the Good or Beautiful Kachina (Wright, page 85).

Shalako Anuthlona, the alternate for Shalako, also called the Shalako Warrior (Wright, page 36).

Koyemshi Awan Tatchu, the Koyemshi Father or Siwuluhsiwa (Wright, page 40).

Kokwele, the Kachina Girl (Wright, page 85).

Shulawitsi An Tatchu, Shulawitsi's ceremonial father (Wright, page 32).

All made by Ravon Chavez.

Courtesy of Turquoise Village

UPPER ROW: Three Shalako Kachinas, the Couriers of the Gods (Wright, page 36), by Ravis Owaleon, Sr.

MIDDLE ROW, *left to right:* Head of the Salimopia Thluptsin'ona, the Yellow Warrior of the North, by Ravis Owaleon, Sr.

Head of the Salimopia Thlian'ona, the Blue Warrior of the West (Wright, page 59), by Ravis Owaleon, Sr.

LOWER ROW, *left to right:* Shulawitsi Kohan'ona, The Little Pekwin or Little Fire God (Wright, page 109), by Ben Seciwa.

Shulawitsi Thlian'ona (Wright, page 109), by Ben Seciwa.

Shulawitsi Shikan'ona (Wright, page 32), wood-carved, by Tiffany Tsabetsaye.

Shulawitsi Shikan'ona (Wright, page 32), by Ben Seciwa.

Shulawitsi Thluptsin'ona (Wright, page 109), by Ben Seciwa..

Courtesy of Turquoise Village

THE SHALAKO CEREMONY, *left to right:*

Shulawitsi, the Little Pekwin or Little Fire God.

Saiyatasha, the Rain Priest of the North or Long Horn.

Yamuhakto, the Wood Carrier.

Hututu, Saiyatasha's Deputy or Pekwin.

Yamuhakto, the Wood Carrier (All of the above, Wright, page 32).

Six Shalako Kachinas, the Couriers of the Gods (Wright, page 36).

Made by Felino Eriacho. This set won First Prize at the Gallup Inter-Tribal Indian Ceremonial in Gallup, New Mexico, in 1994.

Courtesy of Turquoise Village

UPPER ROW, *left to right:* Pasikiapa Mosona, Wide Sleeves Leader (Wright, page 92).

Wakashi, the Cow Kachina (Wright, page 114).

Wakashi Awan Peyenokwe, a Kachina that comes in the Cow Dance and the Mixed Dance asking for songs.

Wilatsukwe Peyenokwe, the Apache Talking Leader (Wright, page 118).

LOWER ROW, *left to right:* Pasikiapa Tese Akenona Okya, Wide Sleeves Pottery Drum Girl (Wright, page 92).

Koyemshi Awan Pekwin, the Speaker of the Sun, is holding corn and piñon nuts (Wright, page 40).

Laguna Chakwaina, also called the Drum Chakwaina, or Chahumoawe and Chanokawistowe, the Short-haired Chakwaina (Wright, page 103).

Hemokatsiki or Ahe'a, the grandmother of all the Kachinas (Wright, page 57).

Kumanshi Domda Caynona, the Comanche Drummer (Wright, page 121).

All made by Ferdinand Waatsa. *Courtesy of Milford Nahohai*

UPPER ROW, *left to right:* Kianakwe Chief, Kianakwe Mosona or Kiamosona (Wright, page 76).

Thlelashoktipona or Wooden Ears (Wright, page 63).

Suyuki (Wright, page 29).

Upo'yona, Pautiwa's son (Wright, page 85).

LOWER ROW, *left to right:* Salimopia Thluptsin'ona, the Yellow Warrior of the North (Wright, page 59).

Salimopia Itapanahnan'ona, the Many-colored Warrior of the Zenith (Wright, page 59).

Salimopia Thlian'ona, the Blue Warrior of the West (Wright, page 59).

All made by Ben Seciwa. *Courtesy of Turquoise Village*

ALL WOOD-CARVED, *left to right:*

Shalako (Wright, page 36) with Saiyatasha, the Rain
Priest of the North or Long Horn (Wright, page 32).
This won First Prize at the Gallup Inter-Tribal
Indian Ceremonial in Gallup, New Mexico,
in 1994.

Nahalilsh' Okya, the Corn Dance Girl
(Wright, page 122).

Nahalilsh' Okya (Wright, page 122).

Shalako (Wright, page 36). This won Second Place
at the Third Annual American Indian Art Festival
and Market in Dallas, Texas, and also Second Place
at the SWAIA Annual Indian Market in Santa Fe,
New Mexico, in 1992.

A:chi'ya'ladaba, Knifewing, a mystic figure.

Shalako (Wright, page 36).

Hututu, Saiyatasha's Deputy or Pekwin
(Wright, page 32).

All made by Felino Eriacho. *Courtesy of Turquoise Village*

ALL WOOD-CARVED, *left to right:*

Tone-ah or Dóna, the Turkey Kachina (Wright,
page 101). *Courtesy of Running Bear Zuni Trading Post*

Kianakwe Kohan'ona, White Kianakwe of the
East (Wright, page 76). *Courtesy of Running Bear Zuni
Trading Post*

Shalako, the Courier of the Gods (Wright, page 36)
with Koyemshi Posuki, the Pouter (Wright, page 41).
Courtesy of Running Bear Zuni Trading Post

Nahalisho, the Corn Dancer (Wright, page 122).
Courtesy of Running Bear Zuni Trading Post

Knifewing or A:chi'ya'ladaba, a mystic figure.
Courtesy of Turquoise Village

Whobone Shelowa, the Santa Domingo Kokokshi
(Wright, page 87) with Sunflower and Koyemshi
Posuki, the Pouter (Wright, page 41).
Courtesy of Turquoise Village

Kokokshi, the Good or Beautiful Kachina (Wright,
page 85) with Koyemshi Posuki, the Pouter (Wright,
page 41). *Courtesy of Turquoise Village*

All made by Tiffany Tsabetsaye.

UPPER ROW, *left to right:* Hehe'a, the Blunderer (Wright, page 72).

Hemokatsiki or Ahe'a, the grandmother of all the Kachinas (Wright, page 57).

Anahoho (Wright, page 63).

Upikaiapona, Downy Feathers Hanging Kachina (Wright, page 87).

LOWER ROW, *left to right:* Atoshle (Wright, page 28).

Salimopia Shelow'ona, the Red Warrior of the South (Wright, page 59).

Saiyathlia Puhu-atinakwe, Blue Horn Warrior God of the Apithlashiwanni (Wright, page 23).

All made by Ben Seciwa. *Courtesy of Turquoise Village*

Pottery

THE ART OF pottery-making was and is dynamic. It has changed periodically over the years. However, some basic factors remain the same: gathering the clay, mixing the clay, and curing the clay. Forming shapes by the hand-coiling method followed, then painting with watered white clay slips. This was followed by carving, stone polishing, and firing. It was a process that brought the potter together with the materials of the earth. It was a bonding link between the people and their land. This process has continued to the present day.

OPPOSITE, *clockwise from upper left:* Pot with rainbird design.

Pot with Matsayka Long-haired Kachina or Upikaiapona Kachina (Wright, page 87).

Pot with Matsayka feather design.

All made by Randy Nahohai.
Courtesy of Pueblo of Zuni Arts & Crafts

Historic Zuni pottery, the pottery of the nineteenth century, was prolific. Potters made food bowls, ceremonial vessels, and bird representations. The pottery was painted in red and black or brown. There has been a great demand for these coveted pieces of pottery by collectors and museums.

Polychrome pottery was introduced by the Zunis around 1910. It was painted with three or more colors or tones, which made up the color scheme. There was widespread use of sculptured frog figures on the jar at the top; painted frogs, tadpoles, and water bug design elements; and feathered serpent images. There were also butterfly designs and deer with heart-line figures.

Shortly after the year 1900, the excellence of Zuni pottery-making began to decline. Vessel walls became thicker, and cooler firing periods robbed the pots of their predecessors' strength.

By 1940 the output was limited. Why did pottery-making in Zuni decline? Even though traditional forms and designs were continued, production levels plummeted in favor of jewelry-making. Silversmithing was far more remunerative than pottery-making. Those potters who were capable of mastering jewelry-making abandoned the ceramic arts in huge numbers. Jewelry-making dominated the Zuni economic scene. However, Zuni pottery survived because important social uses existed that were separate from the outside market. Vessels were potted for cooking, to carry water, and to store food safely. However, pottery began a resurgence in the late 1970s and 1980s.

It was two non-Zuni women who were instrumental in giving a big lift to Zuni pottery-making. Daisy Nampeyo Hooee was a Hopi who married Sidney Hooee, a Zuni. Her grandmother was the legendary Nampeyo, the Hopi-Tewa potter. Daisy learned by constantly watching her grandmother and absorbing her techniques. She still painted in her grandmother's style, but she used Zuni designs from the prehistoric period. She taught the Zuni children the ideas and stories that came from that period and told them to use them.

Jennie Laate, an Acoma potter, married Noel Laate, a Zuni. She joined with Daisy in making pottery in the late 1970s. She was the only artist displaying Zuni pottery at the 1979 Santa Fe Indian Market.

The two women were able to get federal grants for the Zuni High School art program. In the fall of 1976 Jennie was teaching seventy-eight students in six different classes. Both Daisy and Jennie brought with them their backgrounds in pottery-making—imaginative Hopi polychrome painting, and the fine, thin wall of the Acoma tradition. However, the Zuni designs were first and foremost in the teaching and learning process. The students began copying. The copying led to their own interpretations of what the designs really meant.

The process of making pottery, as taught by Daisy and Jennie and generations of potters before them, begins with finding the clay. Zuni potters use local clays. The clay is dried for a day or two and then soaked in buckets of water for about a week until the water has a milky color. It is then screened or sieved to get rid of small rocks and any other extraneous matter. Then the potter adds a temper of sand or finely ground rock or pottery shards. (Pure clay is not used because the pots will crack as they dry and shrink.) The dry clay and tempering material are crushed with a hand stone in order to mix them. When the clay and temper are sufficiently pounded, they are mixed with water to make a paste. Then the mixture is kneaded. The amount of tempering material added is never measured; it is left to the judgment of the potter whose inner sense and experience indicate the stopping point. There has to be enough temper to prevent the vessel from cracking when it is sun-dried but not enough to cause the vessel to crumble or fall apart.

The vessel is built up with rolls of clay applied spirally to obtain the desired size and shape. This is known as the coil method. The surface is then smoothed with a molding tool. The inside of the vessel is also rubbed with a piece of gourd or shell, so that it, too, is smooth. Both the inside and outside are rubbed smooth, wiping out all traces of the coils of clay. The vessel is then set aside to dry in the sun or in the house oven with a slow fire.

After the initial drying period the potter

applies a white slip to the vessel. The white slip is polished with a rubbing stone. The red and black design is painted with a yucca leaf branch that the potter has chewed to the desired thickness. Zuni pottery has primarily white or buff backgrounds. The designs are in black, brown, red, and orange. Native plants and minerals are used to create colors and designs.

The decoration on the body of a Zuni vessel is usually arranged in four panels, alternately wide and narrow. The wide panels, usually more innovative, contain designs of the heart-line deer, the Deer in His House design, a line of small red birds, a rosette (a sacred medallion), or stair-step figures with cross-hatched filling. The potters invariably include a ceremonial break into every line that would otherwise have encircled the pot. Modern potters have suggested this is a path for the spirit to enter and leave or a safeguard against trapping the potter's spirit into the vessel. Potter Randy Nahohai believes that the line is a representation of his own life. If you joined the line together it meant you ended your life. Daisy Hooee felt the line break had to do with long life, children, and healthy people. Some women potters left the line open if they could still bear children or closed it if they could not.

There is much symbolism in the pottery designs. Since Zuni Pueblo is located in a largely arid region, animals associated with water or the seasonal rainfall are predominantly featured. During their migration the Zuni people were searching for the center of the universe and the deer led them to the body of water. Tadpoles, dragonflies, and frogs are symbolic of the rains. The rainbird figure is used to represent rain from a summer storm. Potter Milford Nahohai believes the design represents the rain-bearing cumulus clouds seen in profile as they roll into the Zuni Valley. The leading edges of the clouds produce a curve that looks like a bird's beak. This may have been the origin of the term "rainbird." Hatching or hachure, the drawing of fine parallel lines, is decorative and also symbolic of falling rain.

Another design produced by Zuni potters is a cloud bowl, which is terraced. The terraces simulate the shape of Zuni altars. The potters also create fetish pots, jars that act as houses for fetishes. These feature holes so that the fetishes can be fed, sometimes with cornmeal or food from the table. Zuni potters also make representations of deer with a red heart-line leading from the mouth to the torso. Whether the deer face right or left, the potter creates a strong feeling of movement that emphasizes the horizontal nature of the design. This is called the Deer in His House design.

The vessels that are ready for firing are placed in a hand-constructed oven outdoors when there are no winds to whip the fire out of control or create smudges on the surfaces. The ground must be flat, level, dry, and clean. The sheep manure used for fuel is also dry. Other fuels used are bark, local coal chunks, and wood chips from cedar or juniper trees. The fire is built, and then the sheep manure, flat pieces of broken pottery, and pieces of sheet metal are arranged to make a level floor on which to place the pottery vessels. There is a space above the pottery to allow the fire to get to all surfaces. Large pieces of sheet metal or broken pottery are placed all around the pots to protect them from the flames and burning fuel. Fuel is piled up, completely covering the structure. The firing usually lasts about an hour. After the fire burns itself out and the manure turns to ashes, the pots are removed with sticks or a pitchfork, placed in a pan, and brought into the house to cool. The cooling process takes many hours. If the potter has done a successful firing, the pots will give off a clear tone when tapped.

Today, however, 90 percent of the vessels are kiln-dried. Quanita and Jack Kalestewa are among the few Zuni potters who fire outdoors because they have their own sheep and can use the sheep manure for firing. Sheep manure is better and more efficient than horse or cow manure. The Nahohai family of potters—Josephine, Milford, Randy, and Rowena Him—use a kiln, but they will fire outdoors in the traditional way when they can get the manure.

If you are interested in buying pottery, balance the pot in the palm of one hand and tap it lightly with your knuckle. It should produce a nice ring. If the piece does not ring, it may be cracked or poorly fired. However, plates, ashtrays, and figurines, due to their shape, will not ring.

It is important to remember that old is not necessarily good. The Indian artists today have better tools, better training, and a better sense of themselves and their historic and artistic past than ever before.

Your eye will tell you if the shape is pleasing and symmetrical, the design artistic, the finish smooth. Buy what you like best, what you will enjoy for years to come. Pottery will bring beauty into the home.

The Zuni potters today, though not many in number, are women and men who produce pottery that is utilitarian, ceremonial, and beautiful. The pottery represents history, telling of the way life was in the past and is today. Each pot tells the potter's story. Each pot holds part of the artist's spirit. Each pot is a mirror of life.

FROM YEARS PAST:

Pottery, late 1800s, and cloth doll, 1938, artists unknown. *Courtesy of Beverly Vander Wagen Hurlbut*

Clockwise from upper left: Pot with rainbirds, rosette, and Deer in His House design, by Jennie Laate.
Courtesy of Roxanne and Greg Hofmann

Pot with rainbirds and Deer in His House design, by Quanita Kalestewa.
Courtesy of Roxanne and Greg Hofmann

Small pot with Deer and heart-line, by Kevin Chopito.
Courtesy of Turquoise Village

Pot with rainbirds, rosette, and Deer in His House design, by Jennie Laate.
Courtesy of Roxanne and Greg Hofmann

Pot with three frogs and two plumed serpents (Kolowisi, see Wright, page 55), by Quanita Kalestewa.
Courtesy of Turquoise Village

Pot with rainbirds, rosette, and Deer in His House design, by Jennie Laate.
Courtesy of Roxanne and Greg Hofmann

Left to right: Fetish pot with eight bears on the outside and two bears on the inside.

Fetish pot with eight bears on the outside and four bears on the inside. Stones on the backs of the fetishes are various kinds of serpentine, alabaster, and marble. Both made by Edna Leki.
Courtesy of Turquoise Village

Clockwise from left: Pot with birds, feathers, scrolls, rainbirds, vegetation, Deer in His House design, and Zuni villages on rim, by Noreen Simplicio. This won Third Prize at the Gallup Inter-Tribal Indian Ceremonial in Gallup, New Mexico, in 1992. *Courtesy of Roxanne and Greg Hofmann*

Pot with rainbird, rosette (a sacred Zuni medallion), Deer in His House design, and Zuni village on rim, by Noreen Simplicio.

Courtesy of Roxanne and Greg Hofmann

Pot with designs from Matsayka, the first of Zuni's seven villages, and Hawikuh, the first village that came in contact with the Europeans, by Randy Nahohai. *Courtesy of Pueblo of Zuni Arts & Crafts*

UPPER ROW, *left to right:* Pot with three lizards, feather, scroll, and Deer in His House design, by Priscilla Peynetsa.

Pot with feather, scroll, and Deer in His House design, by Priscilla Peynetsa.

LOWER ROW, *left to right:* Pot with frogs and tadpoles, by Priscilla Peynetsa.

Pot with three lizards, by Rowena Him.

A pot with four Kokopellis, by Randy Nahohai.

Courtesy of Pueblo of Zuni Arts & Crafts

UPPER ROW, *left to right:* Pot with frogs, dragonflies, and cattails, by Marcus Homer. This won First Prize at the Gallup Inter-Tribal Indian Ceremonial in Gallup, New Mexico, in 1994.

Pot with frogs, tadpoles, and dragonflies, by Priscilla Peynetsa.

MIDDLE ROW, *left to right:* Pot with lizards and frogs, by Agnes Peynetsa.

Pot on top, with frogs, by Priscilla Peynetsa.

Pot on bottom, with frogs and tadpoles, by Jack Kalestewa.

Pot with frogs, by Quanita Kalestewa.

LOWER ROW, *left to right:* Pot with frog and design, by Eileen Yatsattie.

Pot with lizards and frogs, by Agnes Peynetsa.

Pot with lizard, by Avelia and Anderson Peynetsa.

All courtesy of Turquoise Village, except pot at lower right, courtesy of Running Bear Zuni Trading Post.

EFFIGY POTTERY OWLS, *top to bottom:*

LEFT: Owl with baby owls on wings, by Quanita Kalestewa.

Owl, by Erma Kalestewa.

CENTER: Three owls, by Erma Kalestewa.

RIGHT: Owl, by Quanita Kalestewa.

Owl, by Irma Nahohai.

Owl, by Quanita Kalestewa.

Courtesy of Pueblo of Zuni Arts & Crafts

Left to right: Effigy owl with five baby owls on the wings, by Quanita Kalestewa.
Courtesy of Pueblo of Zuni Arts & Crafts

Canteen duck with butterfly and Deer in His House design, by Priscilla Peynetsa and Daryl Westika. *Private collection*

Canteen owl, by Rowena Him.
Courtesy of Pueblo of Zuni Arts & Crafts

Canteen duck, by Avelia and Anderson Peynetsa.
Courtesy of Turquoise Village

Clockwise from upper right: Pot with Hawikuh design, by Jack Kalestewa.
Courtesy of Pueblo of Zuni Arts & Crafts

Pot with rain, feathers, and Deer in His House design, by Erma Kalestewa.
Courtesy of Pueblo of Zuni Arts & Crafts

Pot with rain and cloud design with rainbirds and rosettes, by Erma Kalestewa.
Courtesy of Pueblo of Zuni Arts & Crafts

Pot with rainbird design, by Jennie Laate.
Courtesy of Roxanne and Greg Hofmann

LEFT: Pot with lizards, scroll, and feather design, by Avelia and Anderson Peynetsa.

CENTER, *top to bottom:* Pot with serpent, frogs, and tadpoles, by Jack Kalestewa.

Pot with frog, serpent, tadpoles, and horned toad, by Jack Kalestewa.

RIGHT, *top to bottom:* Pot with Deer in His House design, by Jack Kalestewa.

Cornmeal bowl with frog and four Kokopellis on the side, by Randy Nahohai.

Courtesy of Pueblo of Zuni Arts & Crafts

Clockwise from top: Stew bowl with feathers, scroll, and rosette design. *Courtesy of Running Bear Zuni Trading Post*

Pot with lizards. *Courtesy of Ralph Singleton and Frances Snyder*

Pot with lizards. *Courtesy of Judy Johnsen*

All made by Lorenda and Deldrick Cellicion.

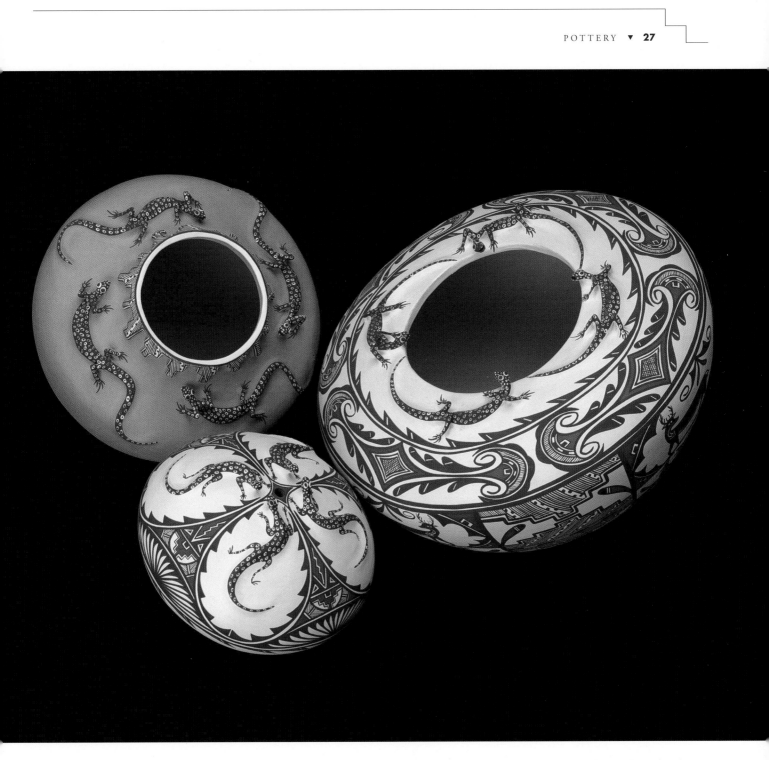

Clockwise from upper left: Pot with lizards and rain and clouds. *Courtesy of Roxanne and Greg Hofmann*

Pot with lizards, Deer in His House Design, feathers, and rain and clouds. *Courtesy of Dan Ostermiller*

Pot with lizards, rain and clouds, and feathers. *Private collection*

All made by Noreen Simplicio.

UPPER ROW, *left to right:* Pot with frogs and dragonflies, by Randy Nahohai.
Courtesy of Turquoise Village

Canteen with frogs, rain clouds, feathers, and vegetation, by Marjorie Esalio.
Courtesy of Turquoise Village

Pot with Matsayka cloud design, by Rowena Him.
Courtesy of Pueblo of Zuni Arts & Crafts

LOWER ROW, *left to right:* Three clay flutes in the shape of frogs, by Randy Nahohai.
Courtesy of Pueblo of Zuni Arts & Crafts

Clockwise from upper left: Deer with heart-line, mountains, and lightning, by Randy Nahohai.
Courtesy of Pueblo of Zuni Arts & Crafts

Scrolls, rainbirds, and feathers, by Rowena Him.
Courtesy of Pueblo of Zuni Arts & Crafts

Matsayka and feather design, by Randy Nahohai. This won Second Prize at the Zuni Show at the Museum of Northern Arizona in Flagstaff in 1990. *Courtesy of Roxanne and Greg Hofmann*

Matsayka cloud and rain design, by Randy Nahohai. *Courtesy of Pueblo of Zuni Arts & Crafts*

A group of miniatures ranging in size from 1½ in. to 3½ in. high. Artists are Marcus Homer, Erma Kalestewa, Agnes Peynetsa, and Eileen Yatsattie.

Courtesy of Pueblo of Zuni Arts & Crafts and Turquoise Village

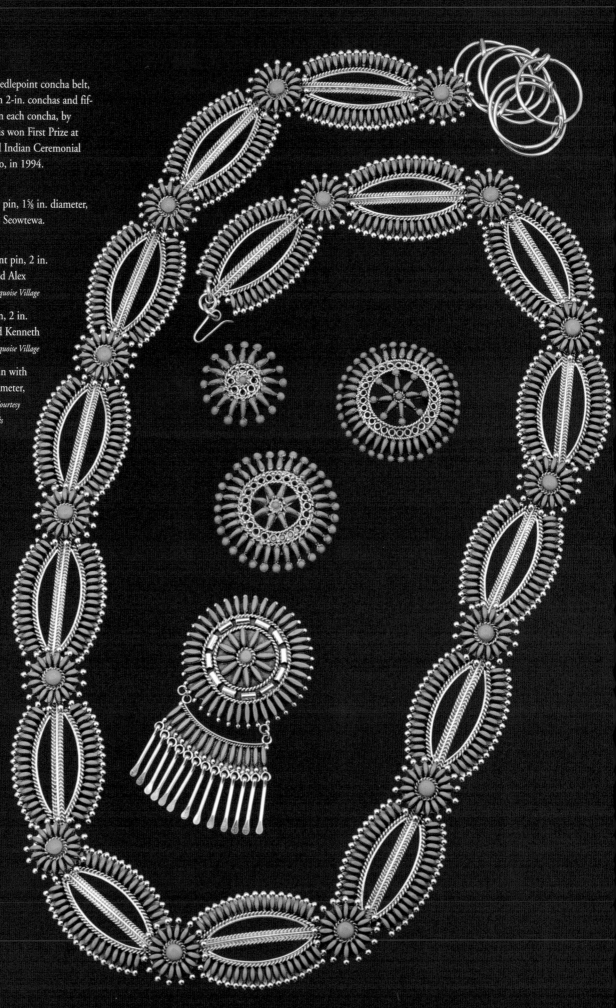

OUTSIDE: Turquoise needlepoint concha belt, 49 in. long with fifteen 2-in. conchas and fifteen flowers in between each concha, by Daryl Fambrough. This won First Prize at the Gallup Inter-Tribal Indian Ceremonial in Gallup, New Mexico, in 1994. *Courtesy of Turquoise Village*

UPPER LEFT: Petit point pin, 1⅝ in. diameter, by Selina and Kenneth Seowtewa. *Courtesy of Turquoise Village*

UPPER RIGHT: Petit point pin, 2 in. diameter, by Odelle and Alex Seowtewa. *Courtesy of Turquoise Village*

CENTER: Petit point pin, 2 in. diameter, by Selina and Kenneth Seowtewa. *Courtesy of Turquoise Village*

LOWER: Needlepoint pin with silver dangles, 2 in. diameter, by Libert Peyketewa. *Courtesy of Pueblo of Zuni Arts & Crafts*

All turquoise is Sleeping Beauty.

Jewelry

IT IS ESTIMATED that of the Zuni's tribal membership of nearly nine thousand, approximately thirty percent handcraft jewelry. Frequently, it is a family or household affair, with children pitching in, helping at first with easier, lesser-skilled tasks. The family works in one of the rooms in the house at a table near a window. Or the household group works in a trailer next to the house.

Between 1830 and 1840, the Zunis made crude jewelry from copper and brass. They broke up old pots and kettles, then melted and pounded them into rather primitive rings, bracelets, and buttons.

In 1872 Atsidi Chon, a Navajo silversmith, visited the Zuni Pueblo. He taught silversmithing to a Zuni named Lanyade. Lanyade was the only Zuni in the Pueblo who was able to speak and understand Navajo.

By the 1890s the Zunis were ready to try the difficult feat of stone setting. They were successful in doing this; it was an accomplishment of far-reaching artistic and economic significance. From 1900 on, the turquoise and silver combination became part and parcel of the jewelry market. Better tools were developed. Jewelry-makers used emery wheels instead of the sandstone slab. They used lapidary sticks tipped with sealing wax to hold the stone against the wheel.

What styles and techniques did the Zunis develop? They emphasized the use of stones and shells, a primary part of their designs. The use of silver was secondary, being the means by which the stones and shells were held in place. Silver was also the preferred material for wire, decorative drops, and ornamental balls.

At first jewelry-making was a joint effort between the Navajos and the Zunis. The Navajos did the silverwork for which they were noted, and the Zunis did the stone and/or shell setting. Then, at a later date, the Zunis worked with both the silver and the stones. As the Zunis became more involved in the making of the jewelry, the Zuni women, usually the wives, became part of the process. Husband and wife teams proliferated.

The first woman jeweler in Zuni was Della Casi, who was taught by her husband in 1926. Other women followed. By 1938 there were eight women who were completely independent silver and stone workers. These women had accounts in their own names with the traders. Today there are many more women who do the whole process, either alone or with a daughter, son, sister, or brother.

The traders in Zuni supplied and still supply the materials and tools needed to make the jewelry. The traders also furnish the marketplace—galleries, museums, dealers, and collectors.

The Zunis became renowned for developing several different styles. They do cluster work, combining a large group of pear-shaped stones, usually turquoise, which symbolizes life-giving power. Other shapes used are teardrop, round, square-cut, and rectangular. The stones are set in a bezel of silver. A bezel is an enclosure of silver that houses the stone (or stones), and holds it in place with a commercial adhesive. Cluster work is used to craft concha belts, pins, pendants, rings, squash blossom necklaces, and bracelets.

The overall design patterns of the jewelry are oval, round, and geometric. Mary and Lee Weebothee, along with Alice Quam, became masters of cluster work.

Petit point evolved as a type of cluster work. In this form of lapidary the stones are rounded at one end and pointed at the other end. The stones are set into a silver bezel in various designs and geometric patterns. Usually the stones are turquoise or coral. Petit point designs appear in rings, pins, pendants, bracelets, and earrings. Socorro and Vincent Johnson excel in petit point jewelry.

Needlepoint also evolved as a style, a new form. The turquoise or coral stones are usually very small, slender, and pointed at each end. The artist begins by holding each piece of turquoise on the end of a very thin lapidary stick, then applies heat to sealing wax, used to hold the raw turquoise in place. Once the stones are in position, the artist then meticulously shapes, grinds, and polishes them—a long, arduous, and tedious task.

Both needlepoint and petit point made their appearance in the 1940s. No other pueblo or tribe has equaled the skill of the best Zuni cutters of the delicate, slender needlepoint turquoise. The Zunis favor the use of Sleeping Beauty turquoise mined in Miami, Arizona; Lone Mountain turquoise from Tonopah, Nevada; and Chinese spiderweb turquoise from mainland China.

Among the Zuni lapidarists who work in the needlepoint style, Irma and Octavius Seowtewa do extraordinary work. First and foremost, however, is Edith Tsabetsaye, who is recognized as the queen of needlepoint. Her work is meticulous, flawless, captivating, and breathtaking.

The Zunis were instrumental in developing another style of jewelry, called inlay. In this style, the stone or shell is cut to fit into channels or grooves in the silver. This is also known as channel work. The precut stones are positioned on the silver base within silver dividers or walls. The stones are glued and then ground until they are flush with the top surfaces of the silver. Nancy and Sheldon Westika, Amy Wesley, and Don Dewa are doing fantastic inlay work.

In etched inlay, a design or picture is etched onto the surface of the stone or silver. The designs include birds, animals, flowers, Koshares, and other figures. Nancy and Dennis Edaakie, Dolly and Albert Banteah, Monica and Harlan Coonsis, and Nancy and Ruddell Laconsello best exemplify this type of inlay, which is considered to be the most difficult inlay technique.

These inlay styles of Zuni jewelry show off an exuberant and abundant use of colored stones and shells. In the past, the Zunis obtained materials from traders: shells from the Gulf of Mexico, turquoise from Cerrillos, New Mexico, and jet from central Mexico. Today Zunis are supplied with red coral from the Mediterranean, yellow shell from Indonesia, spiny oyster shell from Baja California, green snail shell from Greece, pink mussel shell from the Tennessee Valley, turquoise (clear blue and spiderweb) from mainland China. As the demand for fine-colored shells and stones increased, traders further broadened their activities in the world marketplace. Some time later the Zuni artisans began using stones and semi-precious stones such as sugilite,

malachite, and lapis lazuli—even ivory. The Zuni lapidarists knew there was no limit in expressing their artistic goals with the use of these exotic shells, stones, and other materials previously unknown to them.

There is yet another style the Zunis brought into the limelight: the creation of fetish necklaces. Leekya Deyuse is generally credited with being the first of the Zunis in making fetishes for necklaces. From 1920 to 1950 his fetishes were set in silver and sold as fine jewelry. Later on the animal carvings were drilled with holes and strung with heishe. Heishe is a shell that has been cut, drilled, and ground into round pieces. The pieces of heishe are then strung into a necklace with the fetish animals. The animal fetishes generally featured by the Zunis include birds, badgers, beavers, coyotes, ducks, eagles, fish, foxes, horses, moles, mountain lions, owls, parrots, pigs, rams, sheep, squirrels, tadpoles, turtles, wildcats, and wolves. However, the majority of fetish necklaces consists solely of birds.

A variety of stones and shells is used, including the following: amber, coral, cowrie shell, dolomite, gold lip and white mother-of-pearl, green snail shell, fossilized ivory, jet, lapis lazuli, malachite, melon shell, pink coral, pink shell, pipestone, serpentine, spiny oyster shell, sugilite, turquoise, and white clam shell.

Most commonly, the fetish necklaces are strung with olivella shell, turquoise, coral, or penn shell. The Santo Domingo Pueblo in New Mexico is the home of the finest heishe makers, and it is from them the Zunis purchase the finished strands of heishe. The Zuni fetish makers then create a single or multistrand fetish necklace.

The finished product of elegant Santo Domingo heishe and exquisite Zuni carved animals is a sight to behold. It is utterly beautiful. In addition to Leekya Deyuse, other renowned Zuni fetish necklace carvers are Debra Gasper, Dinah and Pete Gasper, Rosita Kaamasee, Rhoda Quam, Andres Quandelacy, and Albenita Yunie.

In addition to the styles described above, some Zunis have crafted in gold, with much of the gold metal visible. The stonework is exquisite, setting off the gold to perfection.

The greatest achievement in jewelry-making at Zuni has been the transition from a craft to fine art. Consequently, Zuni jewelry should be valued for its intrinsic beauty, and recognized for its uniqueness. It should be purchased on its merits as fine jewelry.

NOTE: *All jewelry is sterling silver unless otherwise noted. All gold jewelry is 14-karat unless otherwise noted. All coral is Mediterranean coral.*

IN THE MAKING:

Unfinished and finished pieces showing the process of the making of the jewelry, by Ola and Tony Eriacho. The unfinished shells and stones are turquoise, white mother-of-pearl, coral, and jet.

Courtesy of the artists

IN THE MAKING:

Unfinished and finished bola tie of the White Warrior of the East, Salimopia Kohan'ona (Wright, page 59), by Edward Beyuka. Shells and stones are, left, clockwise from knee of Kachina, gold lip mother-of-pearl, penn shell, turquoise; right, top to bottom, jet, black mother-of-pearl with malachite on top, and black mother-of-pearl with coral on top.

Courtesy of Turquoise Village

FROM YEARS PAST, *clockwise from top:*

Jewelry box made of sterling silver, studded with Lone Mountain turquoise, 3½ in. high and 6 in. diameter. The box was made by Navajo silversmith Joe Yazzie, and the stones set by Mary and Lee Weebothee. This won the Grand Prize Award at the 21st Annual Navajo Tribal Fair in Window Rock, Arizona, in 1967 and First Prize at the Gallup Inter-Tribal Indian Ceremonial in Gallup, New Mexico, the same year.

Bola tie of Knifewing Dancer on black oyster shell overlaid with white mother-of-pearl, gold lip mother-of-pearl, jet, turquoise, coral, and scalloped silver work, 4¾ in. diameter, made in 1985 by Lambert Homer.

Bola tie of sea serpent, Kolowisi (Wright, page 55), on spiny oyster shell overlaid with white mother-of-pearl, coral, turquoise, and gold lip mother-of-pearl with scalloped silver work, 4 in. diameter, made in 1985 by Lambert Homer. *Courtesy of Roxanne and Greg Hofmann*

Fetish necklace with sixty-nine coral birds strung on coral heishe, by Rosita Kaamasee.
Courtesy of Turquoise Village

Elk pin/pendant inlaid with penn shell and fossilized ivory, with outside trim of turquoise and coral, by Margie Ghahate.
Courtesy of Pueblo of Zuni Arts & Crafts

Blackbird pin/pendant inlaid with jet and coral, and flowers of melon shell with outside trim of turquoise, lapis lazuli, and coral, by Nancy and Ruddell Laconsello. *Courtesy of Turquoise Village*

Two-sided bluebird pendant inlaid with turquoise and white mother-of-pearl, with outside trim of coral, by Nancy and Dennis Edaakie.
Ccourtesy of Turquoise Village

FROM YEARS PAST:

LEFT, *top to bottom:* Coral cluster bracelet, made in 1980 by Lolita Wyaco. *Courtesy of Roxanne and Greg Hofmann*

Sun face bracelet with turquoise, coral, jet, and white mother-of-pearl, made in 1968 by Lela and Roger Cellicion. *Private collection*

Knifewing Dancer inlaid pin with red abalone, jet, and white mother-of-pearl, made in 1950s, artist unknown. *Courtesy of Roxanne and Greg Hofmann*

Butterfly inlaid pin/pendant with tortoise shell, turquoise, coral, jet, and white mother-of-pearl, made in 1940, signed BP. *Courtesy of Roxanne and Greg Hofmann*

RIGHT: Inlaid ram bola tie of ram made with white mother-of-pearl, gold lip mother-of-pearl, jet, turquoise, coral, white clam shell, and tortoise shell, made in 1968 by Andrew Dewa. *Private collection*

Fetish necklace with coral, Chinese turquoise, pink shell, spiny oyster shell, and red abalone, by Sarah Leekya. *Courtesy of Turquoise Village*

BRACELETS, *top to bottom:*

LEFT: Ram with Sleeping Beauty turquoise, white mother-of-pearl, coral, and jet, by Sybil Cachini. *Courtesy of Running Bear Zuni Trading Post*

Channel inlay with green snail shell and turquoise, by Orlinda Natewa. This won Third Prize at the Gallup Inter-Tribal Indian Ceremonial in Gallup, New Mexico, in 1994. *Courtesy of Turquoise Village*

Corn Dancer, Nahalisho (Wright, page 122) with turquoise, jet, white mother-of-pearl, malachite, gold lip mother-of-pearl, by Esther and Martin Panteah. *Courtesy of Pueblo of Zuni Arts & Crafts*

Hummingbird inlaid with coral, jet, abalone, penn shell, with flower of turquoise and flower of white mother-of-pearl, by Dolly and Albert Banteah. *Courtesy of Turquoise Village*

Channel inlay with white mother-of-pearl, coral, turquoise, jet, pink mussel shell, and lapis lazuli, by Letitia and Anson Wallace. *Courtesy of Turquoise Village*

Hummingbird inlaid with turquoise, coral, jet, white mother-of-pearl, lapis lazuli, sugilite, malachite, pink mussel shell, and angelite, by Nancy and Ruddell Laconsello. *Courtesy of Turquoise Village*

RIGHT: Carved Sleeping Beauty turquoise, by Robert Eustace. *Courtesy of Turquoise Village*

Channel inlay with turquoise, coral, and jet, by Esther and Martin Panteah. *Courtesy of Pueblo of Zuni Arts & Crafts*

Split needlepoint with turquoise and coral, by Ed Cooeyate. *Courtesy of Running Bear Zuni Trading Post*

Channel inlay with Sleeping Beauty turquoise, by Orlinda Natewa. *Courtesy of Turquoise Village*

Inlay with coral, turquoise, jet, and white mother-of-pearl, by Rachel Tzunie. *Courtesy of Pueblo of Zuni Arts & Crafts*

Raised turquoise, coral, jet, white mother-of-pearl, and abalone, by Matilda and Valentino Banteah. *Courtesy of Pueblo of Zuni Arts & Crafts*

LEFT: Butterfly choker, earrings, ring, and bracelet inlaid with white mother-of-pearl, coral, jet, and turquoise, by Reyes Neha.

RIGHT: Split needlepoint choker and earrings of turquoise and coral with silver dangles, by Ed Cooeyate. These won Third Prize at the Gallup Inter-Tribal Indian Ceremonial in Gallup, New Mexico, in 1994.

Courtesy of Turquoise Village

Red coral cluster concha belt, necklace, earrings, bracelet, and ring, by Alice Quam. Concha belt is 41½ in. long with eight 2¾-in. conchas and a 3⅛-in. buckle. This set won Second Prize at the Gallup Inter-Tribal Indian Ceremonial in Gallup, New Mexico, in 1994.
Courtesy of Turquoise Village

Upper bracelet of Mud Head Kachina, Koyemshi, made of penn shell, coral, white mother-of-pearl, turquoise, and jet, by Beverly Etsate. Lower bracelet, necklace, ring, and two-sided pendant made of jet, turquoise, coral, white mother-of-pearl, pink mussel shell, serpentine, gold lip mother-of-pearl, and penn shell, by Rosalie Pinto. The Kachinas on the necklace are, counter-clockwise from top left: Koshare, Ram, Corn Dancer, Koyemshi, and Ram.

Courtesy of Pueblo of Zuni Arts & Crafts

LEFT : Necklace, earrings, ring, and bracelet inlaid with white mother-of-pearl, jet, and turquoise, by Sonny Wallace.

RIGHT: Necklace, earrings, ring, and bracelet inlaid with pink mussel shell and turquoise, by Fletcher Ahiyite.

Courtesy of Pueblo of Zuni Arts & Crafts

SOMETHING DIFFERENT:

LEFT: Necklace, earrings, and ring made of Chinese turquoise, by Ric Laselute. *Courtesy of Running Bear Zuni Trading Post*

CENTER, *top to bottom:* Pin made of amethyst by Patsy Weebothee. *Courtesy of Pueblo of Zuni Arts & Crafts*

Multicolor cluster pin/pendant with silver dangles, made of red coral, pink coral, Chinese turquoise, Sleeping Beauty turquoise, jet, azurite, sugilite, spiny oyster shell, malachite, variscite, and lapis lazuli by Patsy Weebothee. *Courtesy of Running Bear Zuni Trading Post*

Multicolor dome ring made of malachite, coral, sugilite, white mother-of-pearl, lapis lazuli, pink mussel shell, and melon shell by Darlene Weebothee. *Courtesy of Running Bear Zuni Trading Post*

Ring of Indian chief inlaid with white mother-of-pearl, turquoise, coral, jet, serpentine, and abalone, by Valentino Laweka. *Courtesy of Pueblo of Zuni Arts & Crafts*

RIGHT: Burning Sun pin/pendant inlaid with turquoise, lapis lazuli, coral, amber, and gold lip mother-of-pearl, by Monica and Harlan Coonsis. *Courtesy of Running Bear Zuni Trading Post*

Bola tie of Indian chief with sun face made of turquoise, melon shell, white clam shell, conch shell, coral, gold lip mother-of-pearl, and jet, by Amos Pooacha. *Courtesy of Running Bear Zuni Trading Post.*

SOMETHING DIFFERENT, *clockwise from left:*

Bola tie of lizard overlaid with Sleeping Beauty turquoise and malachite, by Verdie Booqua.
Courtesy of Running Bear Zuni Trading Post

Bola tie inlaid with Sleeping Beauty turquoise, sugilite, malachite, and gold lip mother-of-pearl, by Leola Yuselew. *Courtesy of Turquoise Village*

Necklace, ring, and earrings with Chinese turquoise and white clam shell, by Ric Laselute.
Courtesy of Running Bear Zuni Trading Post

Pin/pendant of Ahmetolela Kachina, the Rainbow Dancer (Wright, page 127), with Chinese turquoise and white clam shell, by Monica and Harlan Coonsis. *Courtesy of Running Bear Zuni Trading Post*

SUN FACES, *from left to right:*

Necklace and earrings inlaid with jet, coral, turq-uoise, and white mother-of-pearl, by Jennifer Lonjose. This set won Second Prize at the Gallup Inter-Tribal Indian Ceremonial in Gallup, New Mexico, in 1994. *Courtesy of Turquoise Village*

Bracelet inlaid with coral, pink coral, turquoise, white mother-of-pearl, fossilized ivory, malachite, sugilite, jet, and lapis lazuli, by Diane and Stanford Cooche.

Courtesy of Running Bear Zuni Trading Post

Bracelet, necklace, and earrings inlaid with white mother-of-pearl, turquoise, coral, and jet, by Vivian and Derrick Hattie.

Courtesy of Turquoise Village

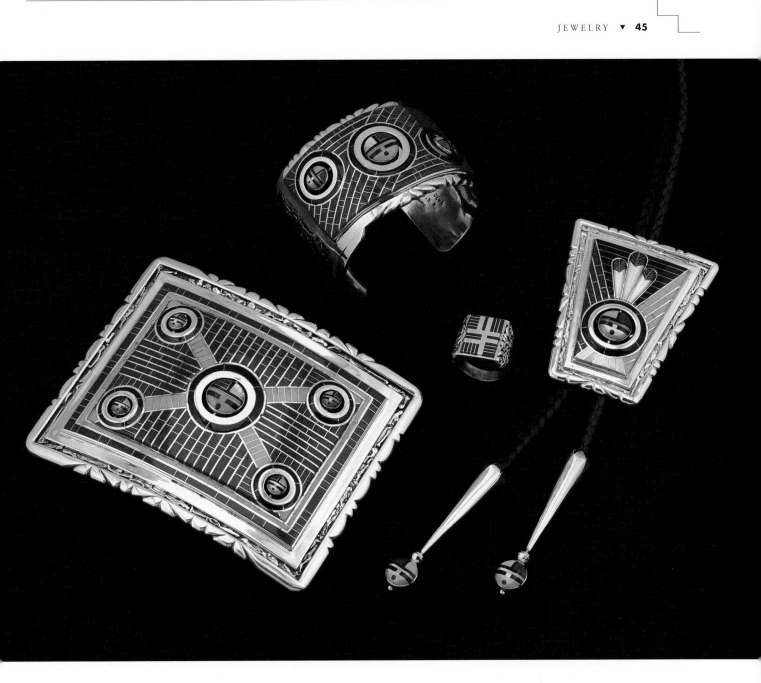

REVOLVING SUN FACES, *clockwise from left:*

Belt buckle, 4 in. x 5 in., and bracelet inlaid with coral, turquoise, white mother-of-pearl, and jet with drop silver, by Don Dewa. *Courtesy of Al Myman*

Bola tie inlaid with coral, turquoise, white mother-of-pearl, gold lip mother-of-pearl, jet, and drop silver, by Don Dewa. *Courtesy of Running Bear Zuni Trading Post*

Ring inlaid with coral and drop silver, by Jeanelle and Samuel Tsalate. *Courtesy of Turquoise Village.*

SUN FACES:

Concha belt, necklace, and earrings inlaid with coral, turquoise, jet, and white mother-of-pearl, by Jeanelle and Keith Waatsa. The concha belt is 42½ in. long, and each concha is 1¼ in. in diameter with a 1¾-in. buckle.

Courtesy of Turquoise Village

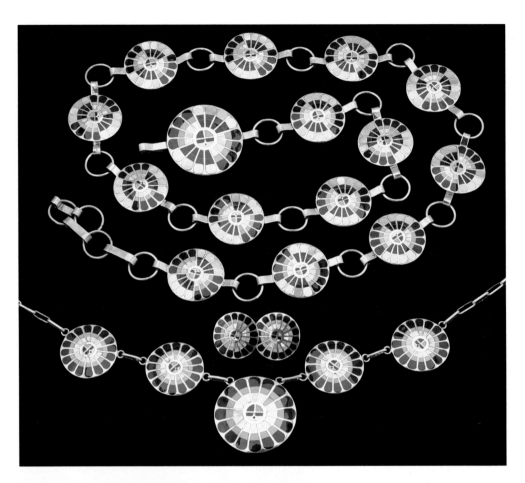

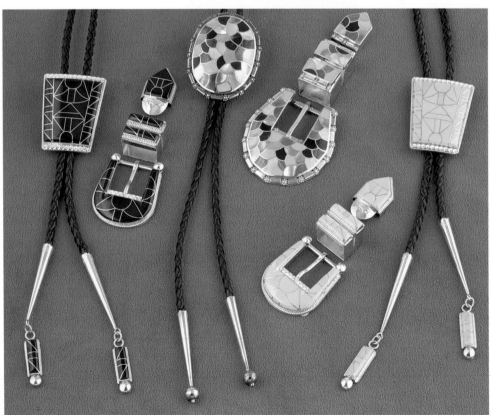

LEFT: Jet channel inlay bola tie and ranger belt buckle, by Diane and Stanford Cooche.

Courtesy of Turquoise Village

CENTER: Channel inlay bola tie and ranger belt buckle made of coral, Sleeping Beauty turquoise, abalone, jet, black mother-of-pearl, malachite, green snail shell, sugilite, pink mussel shell, and white mother-of-pearl, by Carmichael Haloo. *Bola tie courtesy of Running Bear Zuni Trading Post; belt buckle courtesy of Pueblo of Zuni Arts & Crafts*

RIGHT: Turquoise channel inlay bola tie and ranger belt buckle, by Diane and Stanford Cooche.

Courtesy of Turquoise Village

LEFT, *top to bottom:* Knifewing Dancer inlaid with jet, turquoise, coral, gold lip mother-of-pearl, and white mother-of-pearl, by Elizabeth and Adrian Wallace. *Courtesy of Turquoise Village*

Butterfly inlaid with turquoise, coral, gold lip mother-of-pearl, white clam shell, and penn shell, by Oliver Cellicion. *Courtesy of Turquoise Village*

Mokaiapona, Ball-Eyes Kachina (Wright, page 103), inlaid with jet, coral, turquoise, malachite, white mother-of-pearl, and gold lip mother-of-pearl, by Andrea Lonjose Shirley.

Courtesy of Turquoise Village

CENTER, *top to bottom:* Sun face inlaid with turquoise, coral, and jet with turquoise needlepoint stones and silver dangles with jet tips, by Shirley and Benjamen Tzuni. *Courtesy of Turquoise Village*

Thunderbird inlaid with turquoise, coral, jet, white mother-of-pearl, and pink shell, by Delwin Gasper. *Courtesy of Pueblo of Zuni Arts & Crafts*

RIGHT, *top to bottom:* Knifewing Dancer inlaid with turquoise, coral, white clam shell, white mother-of-pearl, and jet, by Esther and Herbert Cellicion.

Courtesy of Turquoise Village

Butterfly inlaid with white mother-of-pearl, gold lip mother-of-pearl, coral, turquoise, jet, and pink shell, by Angela Cellicion. *Courtesy of Turquoise Village*

Salimopia Thlian'ona Kachina, the Blue Warrior of the West (Wright, page 59), inlaid with penn shell, coral, malachite, white mother-of-pearl, and pink shell, by Shirley and Virgil Benn.

Courtesy of Turquoise Village

Bracelets, rings, watch tips, and necklace all inlaid with turquoise, coral, white mother-of-pearl, jet, and gold lip mother-of-pearl, by Ola and Tony Eriacho. *Courtesy of the artists*

Clockwise from bottom: Rainbow man pin/pendant with dangle, inlaid with coral, turquoise, white mother-of-pearl, fossilized ivory, and lapis lazuli, by Monica and Harlan Coonsis.

Rainbow Man pin/pendant inlaid with turquoise, coral, fossilized ivory, jet, white mother-of-pearl, lapis lazuli, and serpentine, by Monica and Harlan Coonsis.

Bird choker inlaid with Sleeping Beauty turquoise, coral, abalone, lapis lazuli, and jet, trimmed with turquoise, white mother-of-pearl, and gold lip mother-of-pearl, by Nancy and Dennis Edaakie.

Knifewing Dancer pin/pendant inlaid with turquoise, coral, gold lip mother-of-pearl, fossilized ivory, abalone, and white mother-of-pearl, by Monica and Harlan Coonsis.

Bluebird pin/pendant inlaid with turquoise, jet, and white mother-of-pearl, flowers with malachite, green turquoise, pink coral, and lapis lazuli, with outside trim of coral, by Nancy and Ruddell Laconsello.

Courtesy of Turquoise Village

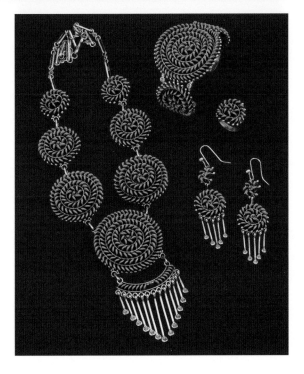

Sleeping Beauty turquoise necklace, bracelet, earrings, and ring with curved needlepoint stones in the shape of a half-moon, by Irma and Octavius Seowtewa. This set won Second Prize at the Gallup Inter-Tribal Indian Ceremonial in Gallup, New Mexico, in 1994.

Courtesy of Turquoise Village

Bracelet, ring, and concha belt made with Sleeping Beauty turquoise, by Bernice and Robert Leekya. Belt has twelve conchas, each 2¼ in. x 1¼ in. The total length without the extra leather at the end is 31 in. *Bracelet courtesy of Turquoise Village, concha belt and ring courtesy of Pueblo of Zuni Arts & Crafts*

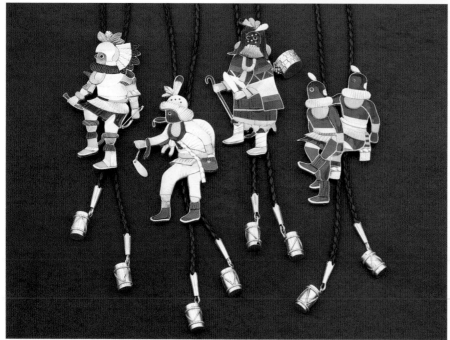

BOLA TIES, *left to right:*

Saiyathlia Tenapikanika Kachina (Wright, page 23) inlaid with turquoise, jet, coral, malachite, abalone, pink mussel shell, gold lip mother-of-pearl, and white mother-of-pearl.

Owiwi or Howiwi Kachina (Wright, page 105) inlaid with turquoise, jet, coral, penn shell, white mother-of-pearl, pink shell, gold lip mother-of-pearl, and abalone.

Suyuki Kachina (Wright, page 29) inlaid with turquoise, coral, jet, penn shell, abalone, white mother-of-pearl, and pink mussel shell.

Ishan Atsan Atshi, the Greasy Boys (Wright, page 96), inlaid with turquoise, coral, jet, penn shell, white mother-of-pearl, gold lip mother-of-pearl, and pink mussel shell.

All made by Edward Beyuka. *Courtesy of Turquoise Village*

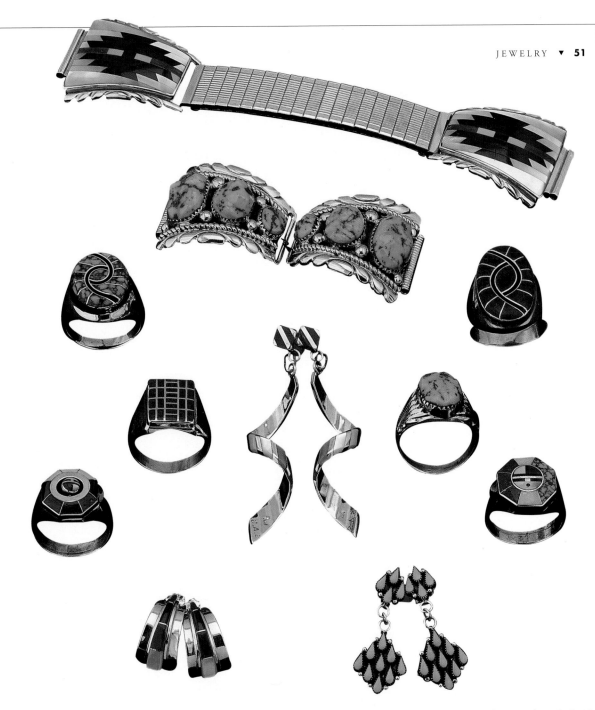

ALL 14-KARAT GOLD:

UPPER ROW: Watch tips inlaid with white mother-of-pearl, jet, turquoise, and coral, by Alfred Dewesee. *Courtesy of Running Bear Zuni Trading Post*

SECOND ROW: Ring with coral channel inlay, by Amy Wesley. *Courtesy of Roxanne and Greg Hofmann*

Watch tips made with Sleeping Beauty turquoise, by Bernice and Robert Leekya. *Courtesy of Turquoise Village*

Channel inlay ring with Chinese turquoise, by Dickie Quandelacy. *Courtesy of Running Bear Zuni Trading Post*

THIRD ROW: Ring of sun face inlaid with jet, turquoise, white mother-of-pearl, and lapis lazuli, by Don Dewa. *Courtesy of Turquoise Village*

Single stone ring with Sleeping Beauty turquoise, by Bernice and Robert Leekya. *Courtesy of Turquoise Village*

Earrings inlaid with turquoise, jet, pink coral, coral, white mother-of-pearl, gold lip mother-of-pearl, and lapis lazuli, by Andrea and Steven Sheyka. *Courtesy of Turquoise Village*

Channel inlay ring with sugilite, by Nancy and Sheldon Westika. *Courtesy of Turquoise Village*

Ring with revolving sun face inlaid with turquoise, coral, jet, white mother-of-pearl, lapis lazuli, and malachite, by Don Dewa. *Courtesy of Turquoise Village*

LOWER ROW: Petit point turquoise earrings, by Patrick Chavez. *Courtesy of Turquoise Village*

Earrings inlaid with sugilite, coral, jet, and abalone, by Rufina and John Cly. *Courtesy of Turquoise Village*

UPPER ROW, *left to right:* Reversible pendant of Koshare Clown inlaid with jet, white mother-of-pearl, coral, and abalone, by Myron Edaakie. *Courtesy of Pueblo Zuni Arts & Crafts*

Belt buckle with Koshare Clown inlaid with white mother-of-pearl, abalone, jet, turquoise, and coral, by Nichelle and Derrick Edaakie. *Courtesy of Turquoise Village*

SECOND ROW, *left to right:* Ring with turquoise channel inlay, by Lydia and Tilden Bowekaty. *Courtesy of Turquoise Village*

Ring of Eagle Dancer inlaid with penn shell, turquoise, coral, pink mussel shell, gold lip mother-of-pearl, and sugilite, by Madeline Beyuka. *Courtesy of Turquoise Village*

Ring of Shalako Kachina, the Courier of the Gods (Wright, page 36), set with turquoise and coral stones, artist unknown. *Courtesy of Turquoise Village*

THIRD ROW, *left to right:* Ring with turquoise channel inlay, by Carmichael Haloo. *Courtesy of Turquoise Village*

Ring of owl inlaid with white clam shell, turquoise, coral, jet, and cowrie shell, by Lulena Esalio. *Courtesy of Pueblo Zuni Arts & Crafts*

Ring of turquoise petit point, by Socorro and Vincent Johnson. This won Second Prize at the Gallup Inter-Tribal Indian Ceremonial in Gallup, New Mexico, in 1994. *Courtesy of Turquoise Village*

LOWER ROW, *left to right:* Ring with Sleeping Beauty turquoise cluster, by Alice Quam. *Courtesy of Turquoise Village*

Triangular ring inlaid with turquoise, coral, white mother-of-pearl, gold lip mother-of-pearl, serpentine, and lapis lazuli, artist unknown. *Courtesy of Pueblo Zuni Arts & Crafts*

Ring of bird inlaid with coral and jet, with flowers of white clam shell, jet, coral, turquoise, and serpentine, and outer rim of turquoise, lapis lazuli, coral, and white clam shell, by Nancy and Ruddell Laconsello. *Courtesy of Turquoise Village*

Lone Mountain turquoise necklace and earrings, by Edith Tsabetsaye. The necklace and earrings have six hundred stones. This set won Best of Class, Best of Category, and First Prize at the Gallup Inter-Tribal Indian Ceremonial in Gallup, New Mexico, in 1993. *Courtesy of Turquoise Village*

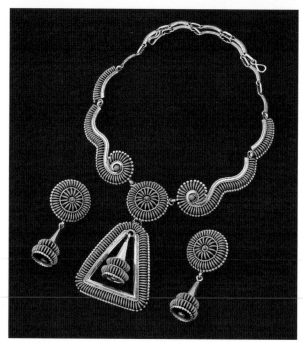

BELT BUCKLES:

LEFT, *top to bottom:* Turquoise, by Mary Ann and Felix Chavez. *Courtesy of Turquoise Village*

Inlaid with turquoise, gold lip and white mother-of-pearl, coral, and jet, by Viola and Donald Eriacho. *Courtesy of Turquoise Village*

CENTER, *top to bottom:* Carved turquoise, by Robert Eustace. *Courtesy of Turquoise Village*

Inlaid with turquoise, coral, white mother-of-pearl, jet, and gold lip mother-of-pearl, by Virginia and

Wayne Quam. This won Second Prize at the Gallup Inter-Tribal Indian Ceremonial in Gallup, New Mexico, in 1994. *Courtesy of Turquoise Village*

Indian chief inlaid with turquoise, red spiny oyster shell, white mother-of-pearl, gold lip mother-of-pearl, penn shell, and fossilized ivory, by Ralph Quam. *Courtesy of Pueblo Zuni Arts & Crafts*

Inlaid with turquoise, coral, white mother-of-pearl, and jet, by Diane Boone. *Courtesy of Pueblo Zuni Arts & Crafts*

RIGHT, *top to bottom:* Rectangular stones of white mother-of-pearl, turquoise, pink coral, and jet, by Esther and Martin Panteah.
Courtesy of Pueblo Zuni Arts & Crafts

Turquoise channel inlay, by Nancy and Sheldon Westika. *Courtesy of Turquoise Village*

All turquoise is Sleeping Beauty.

Beadwork

TODAY, ZUNI CRAFTSPEOPLE who make beaded dolls are happy to be called folk artists. This was not always the case. Back in the 1930s, trading posts, shops, and markets throughout the Southwest sold many beaded curios. These handmade items were extremely inexpensive, and tourists bought them in the thousands as souvenirs to remember their visit to Indian country. Yet these beaded items had distinguishing characteristics: They were unique, and they were made by the elder women of the Zuni tribe. Today, however, they are made by both women and men.

Beadwork originally came to the Zunis through the Plains Indians, with whom they traded as early as the 1700s. The Plains Indians incorporated beaded designs on their saddles, cradleboards, clothing, moccasins, and war bonnets. Though very few Zunis do beadwork today, there has been a growing demand for better crafted beaded dolls. Many trading posts of the Southwest have requests for the more unusual beaded figures, even though they are more expensive than the curio trinkets of the past. The recognition and popularity of beaded folk art has grown. The Zuni beadworkers are being kept busy.

BEADED OWLS:

Ranging in height from 2 in. to 13 in., by Candeloria Cellicion, Claudia Cellicion, and Gloria Cooeyate.

The 13-in. owl is courtesy of Judy Johnsen; the orange, blue, yellow, and turquoise owls are courtesy of Malcolm Maxwell Newman; others are from a private collection

The beads used are imported seed beads from France, glass beads named for their size. The process of making beads goes back one hundred years. Glass beads come in a variety of colors, either opaque or transparent, and the colors are accented from within the glass. The beads are uniform in size, and the holes are drilled in the same place. Shops such as Bovis Beads in Tucson, Arizona, carry seed beads that can be mail-ordered. In Zuni the beadworkers are able to obtain beads at the Pueblo of Zuni Arts & Crafts and the Halona Trading Post.

The early beaded figures featured three styles, which are still made today. They are the Comanche doll, the skirt doll, and the cow head.

Comanche dolls are representations of men in Plains Indian costume, including feather bonnets or headdresses replete with beadwork. To the Zunis, "Comanche" and "Plains Indian" are synonymous. Coincidentally, the Comanche Dance is a popularly performed social dance not only in Zuni, but also in many of the other pueblos.

The skirt dolls are fully skirted, sometimes in two layers. Usually, a rabbit's foot is placed into the doll's body or feet.

The cow heads are made from sheep vertebrae. The beadworker wraps a piece of cloth over the center of the vertebra. The beading is then done on the cloth in a design to simulate the face of a cow. The exposed, unbeaded ends of the bone look like horns. The cow heads are open in the center and are used as neckerchief slides or bola ties.

Today, hundreds of Zunis still make small curio-type beaded work, but only as a means to make extra money. The larger and more skillfully crafted figures are sold to the Pueblo's dealers by a few Zunis who earn their major income from beadwork.

Mabel Ghahate has been beading for over forty years. She specializes in beaded animals—horses, cows, antelope, deer, and sheep. She creatively uses a modified wishbone for a pronghorn antelope and a branching chicken bone to form the antlers of a deer. She also makes Santa Claus figures for special Christmas orders.

Winifred Cowyuka has also been beading for over forty years. She never makes Comanches with rabbits' feet, nor does she make small skirt dolls. She has specialized in larger dolls—four to seven inches high—such as Comanches and Olla Maidens. The Olla Maidens are a group of Zuni women performers who, garbed in traditional costume, carry water jars or ollas balanced on their heads and sing as a group or individually. Winifred has won prizes at the Gallup Inter-Tribal Indian Ceremonial in Gallup, New Mexico.

Claudia Cellicion began beading small curios and has now graduated to larger figures, such as the Olla Maidens. She is responsible for introducing the use of carved wooden foundations or bases for her dolls. Her husband, Todd Poncho, a Kachina doll carver, makes these for her, and even started beading dolls himself. Claudia also makes beaded Navajo Dance figures, Butterfly Dancers, Koshares (Rio Grande clown figures), and other Zuni social dancers.

In the past, Claudia used a thread that was made for beading, but she had trouble with it bunching up. She then found a polyester sewing thread that was available on a spool, and used it successfully. Claudia tries to have one continuous thread for the figure. If the thread should break, she ties the end in a knot and hides it in the beadwork. She has won prizes at the Museum of Northern Arizona's Zuni Show in Flagstaff, Arizona, and at the Gallup Inter-Tribal Indian Ceremonial in Gallup, New Mexico.

Candy Cellicion, sister of Claudia, specializes in Apache Mountain Spirit Dancers and Hopi Snake Dancers. Both Candy and Claudia do beadwork that has a myriad of detail. Their work is bold, vivid, and flamboyant.

What are the signs of good beadwork? The beads should be uniformly smooth. The representation of the storytellers, dancers, or animals should be accurate, and the detailing of the costumes and stances of the subjects should be pleasing to the eye. The use of carved cottonwood bases is innovative and is mainly a feature of the more skilled beadworker. Today Zuni beaded doll work has made the successful journey from curio to respected folk art.

THE OLD AND THE NEW:

UPPER ROW, *left to right:* Zuni woman with pot on head, 9 in. high, made in 1972 by Claudia Cellicion. *Private Collection*

Zuni woman with pot on head, 9½ in. high, by Claudia Cellicion. This won First Prize at the Gallup Inter-Tribal Indian Ceremonial in Gallup, New Mexico, in 1990. *Courtesy of Judy Johnsen*

Navajo woman, 6 in. high, made in 1971 by Anita Mahkee. *Private collection*

LOWER ROW: Two storytellers, 4 in. tall, made in 1993 by Claudia Cellicion. *Private collection and courtesy of Judy Johnsen*

LEFT, *top to bottom:* Eagle Dancer with removable mask, by Claudia Cellicion. *Courtesy of Turquoise Village*

Two Koshare clowns slicing water-melon, by Candeloria Cellicion. *Courtesy of Pueblo of Zuni Arts & Crafts*

Man with drum, by Candeloria Cellicion. *Courtesy of Turquoise Village*

RIGHT, *top to bottom:* Koshare clown holding smaller clown, by Claudia Cellicion. *Courtesy of Turquoise Village*

Small Koshare clown with water-melon, by Claudia Cellicion. *Courtesy of Milford Nahohai*

Three women with drums, by Candeloria Cellicion. *Courtesy of Turquoise Village*

Left to right: Fancy War Dancer, by Claudia Cellicion. *Courtesy of Ralph Singleton and Frances Snyder*

Female Long-Haired Kachina, by Todd Poncho. *Courtesy of Milford Nahohai*

Powwow Dancer, by Claudia Cellicion. *Courtesy of Turquoise Village*

Comanche Dancer, by Winifred Cowyuka. *Courtesy of Turquoise Village*

Hoop Dancer, by Claudia Cellicion. *Courtesy of Milford Nahohai*

Clockwise, from middle left: Brown cow, by Mabel Ghahate. *Courtesy of Milford Nahohai*

Horse, cow, and ram, by Mabel Ghahate. *Courtesy of Pueblo of Zuni Arts & Crafts*

Woman on horse and man on horse, by Effie Boone. *Courtesy of Turquoise Village*

Cow heads, by Gretchen Laate. *Courtesy of Turquoise Village*

UPPER ROW, *left to right:* Santa Claus, by Candeloria Cellicion. *Courtesy of Pueblo of Zuni Arts & Crafts*

Santa Claus, by Claudia Cellicion. *Courtesy of Milford Nahohai*

Santa Claus, by Claudia Cellicion. *Courtesy of Turquoise Village*

LOWER ROW, *left to right:* Snowman, by Claudia Cellicion. *Courtesy of Turquoise Village*

Santa Claus, by Candeloria Cellicion. *Courtesy of Milford Nahohai*

Fetishes

A FETISH IS an animal carving, usually made of stone or shell. It is said to house the spirit or supernatural qualities of that animal. If the fetish is properly fed and nurtured with cornmeal and water, it may bring special power to the people who use it.

Native Americans of different tribes have used animal fetishes in prayers and ceremonies and as talismans and amulets for successful hunting and fishing, procreation, agriculture, health,

protection of the young, and long life. Originally intended to be hunting charms, fetishes have become associated with war, propagation, curing diseases, initiation, and fertility of crops. Fetishes may be tribal or personal in use.

The Zunis think of fetishes as carvings that become fetishes in the true Zuni sense only after they have been blessed by the tribal Medicine Society at the Winter Solstice gathering that takes place in early December each year. The Zunis first used fetishes as early as A.D. 650. The fetishes that have been in tribal or individual possession for centuries are considered the most holy and most valuable.

Zuni fetish carvers maintain that if you believe in the power of the fetish to bring good luck, it probably will. If you do not believe, it

---

UPPER ROW, *left to right:* Alabaster ram, by Rodney Laiwakete.

Serpentine ram, by Derrick Kaamasee.

Ram of ibex horn with turquoise eyes, by Max Laate.

LOWER ROW, *left to right:* Alabaster ram, by Rickson Kallestewa.

Picasso marble ram, by Fabian Cheama.

Courtesy of Pueblo of Zuni Arts & Crafts

probably won't. As a point of interest, a fine Zuni fetish carver said, "In our tradition, fetishes are used for things like healing, protection, spiritual guidance, good luck, and longevity. A lot of my customers believe in that. I believe in that. But in my work I don't guarantee it."

The Zuni fetish carvers are generally acknowledged as doing the finest work among all the tribes of the Southwest. Navajos, for example, will barter for Zuni fetishes of horses, sheep, cattle, or goats in order to keep their herds and flocks free from disease and to insure propagation.

Fascination with fetishes and their powers is timeless. There is no essential difference between a new or an old fetish. The "antiquing" of new fetishes is practiced occasionally by carvers who attempt to simulate the beautiful finish their family has been noted for in past years. A very few carvers may "antique" because they like that appearance, or because a naive non-Indian collector might be inclined to believe that age can be directly equated with quality and value. There is, however, a difference in the quality of the old versus the new. The new Zuni fetish carvings have a higher standard of craftsmanship and beauty, a greater attention to detail, and a greater sophistication in the polishing and finishing.

Fetish carving, like all arts in Zuni, is done in the home. The work is performed by all members of the family—by men and women, along with their children, brothers, or sisters. Because each carver develops a unique style, it is possible to look at a display of several thousand Zuni fetish carvings and pick out the individuals or families who made them. Today most carvers have no other employment unless it is seasonal, such as road building or fire fighting.

The process of carving a fetish begins when the carver saws large chunks of the material to be used into smaller blocks or pieces. Usually the smaller pieces of material will have the correct proportion for the animals being produced. After the material has been cut down to size, the carver uses a grinding wheel to rough the piece into the preliminary shape of the desired figure. The carver refines the shape with another wheel, appropriately called Brite Boy. A buffing compound, Zam, is wiped on the carving and buffed with a muslin cloth or chamois wheel for the final polish. However, some carvers may use emery paper for this process. Then a Dremel, a handheld power tool, is used for cutting details and inlay, such as the eyes and the heart-line. The heart-line leads from the mouth of the fetish animal to the torso and represents the breath of the animal. (This motif is also frequently seen in pottery.) The finished fetish carving is often approximately sixty percent of the original size of block the carver began with.

The Zunis believe there are many fetish animals that bring special powers to the people who use them. They further believe there are six primary directions, with corresponding animals for each direction.

The North is associated with the mountain lion fetish. The mountain lion fetish is used as a talisman for the hunter in the taking of game, such as deer, elk, and buffalo. The mountain lion fetish protects the carriers on their journeys.

The East is represented by the wolf fetish. This fetish has superlative hunting powers especially when the Zuni hunter is looking for antelope.

The South is denoted by the badger fetish and the bobcat fetish. The Zuni uses the bobcat to hunt the antelope. The badger fetish helps medicine men and shamans—priests who use extraordinary powers for the purpose of curing the sick, divining the hidden, and controlling events—to locate healing herbs and roots.

The West is associated with the bear fetish and coyote fetish. The bear fetish has great healing powers and the white bear fetish provides even greater healing qualities. The coyote fetish is used when hunting rabbit.

The Zenith or Up direction is represented by the eagle fetish. Hunters will carry the eagle fetish when rabbits and small game are the prey. This fetish also aids the shaman in diagnosing a patient's illness.

The Nadir or Down direction is symbolized by the mole fetish. This fetish protects growing crops by routing out the rodents that attack plants.

If the fetishes of the six cardinal directions would be created in traditional fashion, they would typically employ the following specific colors:

> *Badger*—red
> *Bobcat*—red
> *Bear*—blue
> *Coyote*—blue
> *Mole*—black
> *Wolf*—white
> *Eagle*—all colors
> *Mountain lion*—yellow

However, in the non-traditional manner, many of the carvers use stones and shells with a huge variety of colors.

The most commonly carved fetishes include: badger, bear, buffalo, coyote, eagle, fox, frog, horned toad, horse, lizard, mole, mountain lion, owl, ram, snake, turtle, and wildcat.

The numerous shells and stones used for fetishes include: alabaster, amber, azurite, coral, cowrie shell, deer antler, dolomite, elk antler, feldspar, fossilized ivory, gold lip mother-of-pearl, green snail shell, jadeite, jet, lapis lazuli, malachite, marble from both Europe and the United States, melon shell, Picasso marble, pink coral, pink shell, pipestone, septarian nodule, serpentine, soapstone, spiny oyster shell, sugilite, travertine, turquoise, and white clam shell.

The raw materials are generally purchased from the trading posts in Zuni, where the finished fetish carvings are generally sold as well.

Turquoise Village, a trading post in Zuni, estimates that they alone buy fifty thousand fetishes a year from the three hundred or so full-time and part-time fetish carvers.

These figures represent a veritable explosion in the fetish market. In years past, the carvers made traditional fetishes with an abstract, simple line quality. Today the younger carvers strive for a detailed and realistic style. Some are even creating miniature sculptures. It is no wonder that the popularity of fetish carvings continues to grow. People are buying not only because they believe that the fetish will protect them, their environment, and their spirituality, but also because of aesthetic considerations. The fetish is an art object that feels good to the touch. It is attractive, and the color and artistry are satisfying. It is handcrafted, with no two exactly the same, and it is generally affordable. The collector can put the fetish in a pouch filled with cornmeal and carry it in a pocket or wear it on a thong around the neck, or keep it in the glove compartment of the car. The fetish can also be placed in a display cabinet or on top of a dresser and viewed as folk art. As such, the highly polished fetish emits a shine and luster that capture the essence of completeness, charm, and beauty.

TURQUOISE FETISHES, OLD AND NEW:

UPPER ROW, *left to right:* Mountain sheep, by David Tsikewa, won First Prize and Special Award in the Gallup Inter-Tribal Indian Ceremonial in Gallup, New Mexico, in 1965.
Courtesy of Roxanne and Greg Hofmann

Bird, Chinese turquoise, made in 1993 by Sarah Leekya. *Courtesy of Turquoise Village*

CENTER ROW, *left to right:* Frog of Castle Dome turquoise, made in 1988 by Dinah and Pete Gasper.
Courtesy of Roxanne and Greg Hofmann

Bear of Chinese turquoise with arrowhead, made in 1990 by Anderson Weahkee.
Courtesy of Roxanne and Greg Hofmann

Frog of Chinese turquoise, made in 1992 by Anderson Weahkee. *Courtesy of Roxanne and Greg Hofmann*

LOWER ROW, *left to right:* Frog of Castle Dome turquoise, made in 1993 by Dinah and Pete Gasper.

Frog of Kingman turquoise, made in 1979 by Dinah and Pete Gasper.
Courtesy of Roxanne and Greg Hofmann

UPPER ROW, *left to right:* Dolomite bear, by Alan Lasiloo. *Courtesy of Pueblo of Zuni Arts & Crafts*

Dolomite bear, by Brian Ahiyite.
Courtesy of Pueblo of Zuni Arts & Crafts

Jadeite bear with turquoise heart-line, by Stuart Quandelacy. *Courtesy of Turquoise Village*

Angelite bear with arrowhead, by Alan Lasiloo.
Courtesy of Turquoise Village

MIDDLE ROW, *left to right:* Alabaster bear, by Alan Lewis. *Courtesy of Pueblo of Zuni Arts & Crafts*

Picasso marble buffalo, by Julius Yuselew.
Courtesy of Pueblo of ZuniArts & Crafts

Onyx bear, by David Chavez. *Courtesy of Turquoise Village*

Picasso marble bear, by Rodney Laiwakete.
Courtesy of Pueblo of Zuni Arts & Crafts

LOWER ROW, *left to right:* Bear of zebra stone, by Annette Tsikewa. *Courtesy of Pueblo of Zuni Arts & Crafts*

Fox of green snail shell with amber arrowhead, by Bernard Homer. *Courtesy of Roxanne and Greg Hofmann*

UPPER ROW, *left to right:* Buffalo of Picasso marble, by Clive Hustito. *Courtesy of Pueblo of Zuni Arts & Crafts*

Bobcat of Picasso marble, by Wilfred Cheama. *Courtesy of Turquoise Village*

SECOND ROW, *left to right:* Frog of green snail shell, by Ricky Laahty. *Courtesy of Roxanne and Greg Hofmann*

Skunk of white mother-of-pearl and jet, made in 1930s by Leekya Deyuse (Old Man Leekya). *Courtesy of Roxanne and Greg Hofmann*

THIRD ROW, *left to right:* Serpentine eagle, by Herb Hustito. *Courtesy of Turquoise Village*

Duck of melon shell with turquoise beak, by Darren Boone. *Courtesy of Pueblo of Zuni Arts & Crafts*

Turtle with sun face of serpentine, coral, turquoise, jet, white mother-of-pearl, and cowrie shell on back, by Fabian Homer. *Courtesy of Turquoise Village*

LOWER ROW, *left to right:* Pipestone frog with turquoise, by Darrin Shebola. *Courtesy of Turquoise Village*

Black marble turtle with turquoise spots, by Todd Etsate. *Courtesy of Pueblo of Zuni Arts & Crafts*

UPPER ROW, *left to right:* Alabaster snake, by Derrick Kaamasee. *Courtesy of Pueblo of Zuni Arts & Crafts*

Picasso marble snake, by Kent Banteah. *Courtesy of Turquoise Village*

Clay snake, artist unknown. *Courtesy of Milford Nahohai*

SECOND ROW, *left to right:* Snake of Sonoran dolomite, by Garrick Weeka. *Courtesy of Turquoise Village*

Snake of deer antler and fur, by Howard Dutukewa. *Courtesy of Turquoise Village*

THIRD ROW, *left to right:* Pipestone snake, by Darrin Shebola. *Courtesy of Turquoise Village*

Wood snake, by Michael Chavez. *Courtesy of Turquoise Village*

Pipestone snake, by Loren Burns. *Courtesy of Turquoise Village*

Wood snake, by Michael Chavez. *Courtesy of Turquoise Village*

LOWER: Argillite snake, by Libert Kaskalla. *Courtesy of Turquoise Village*

ALL DEER ANTLER:

UPPER ROW, *left to right:* Mountain goat and snake; moose and turkey; and dinosaur, all made by Derrick Kaamasee.

Great horned owl with two lizards, by Max Laate.

LOWER ROW, *left to right:* Two baby owls and bird, by Marvelita Phillips.

Owl, by Max Laate.

Coyote with baby eagle, by Estaban Najera.

Turtles, by Max Laate.

Owl, by Derrick Kaamasee.

Rat with leaf, by Max Laate.

All courtesy of Pueblo of Zuni Arts & Crafts except bottom left, courtesy of Turquoise Village

ALL AMBER:

UPPER ROW, *left to right:* Bear with turquoise heart-line, by Andres Quandelacy.
Courtesy of Turquoise Village

Buffalo with turquoise eyes and horns, by Jane Quam.
Courtesy of Turquoise Village

SECOND ROW, *left to right:* Rabbit with turquoise eyes, by Barry Yamutewa.
Courtesy of Turquoise Village

Buffalo with turquoise horns, by Rhoda Quam.
Courtesy of Turquoise Village

Buffalo with turquoise horns, by Rhoda Quam.
Courtesy of Turquoise Village

THIRD ROW, *left to right:* Bear with turquoise, by Rhoda Quam.
Courtesy of Turquoise Village

Bear with turquoise, by Andres Quandelacy.
Courtesy of Pueblo of Zuni Arts & Crafts

LOWER ROW, *left to right:* Bear with turquoise heart-line, mouth, and eyes, by Georgianne Quandelacy.
Courtesy of Turquoise Village

Bear with turquoise heart-line, mouth, and eyes, by Andres Quandelacy.
Courtesy of Pueblo of Zuni Arts & Crafts

UPPER ROW, *left to right:* Orange alabaster bear, by Rickson Kallestewa.
Courtesy of Pueblo of Zuni Arts & Crafts

Orange alabaster bear with turquoise heart-line, by Albenita Yunie. *Courtesy of Turquoise Village*

SECOND ROW, *left to right:* Travertine skunk with shell arrowhead, by Loren Leekela.
Courtesy of Pueblo of Zuni Arts & Crafts

Serpentine bear with shell arrowhead, by Stuart Quandelacy. *Courtesy of Turquoise Village*

THIRD ROW, *left to right:* Malachite bear, by Jimmy Yawakia. *Courtesy of Turquoise Village*

Jet bear with turquoise arrowhead, by Rodney Laiwakete. *Courtesy of Pueblo of Zuni Arts & Crafts*

Picasso marble bear with shell arrowhead, by Brian Ahiyite. *Courtesy of Turquoise Village*

LOWER ROW, *left to right:* Pipestone bear with turquoise fish and arrowhead, by Jeff Eriacho.
Courtesy of Pueblo of Zuni Arts & Crafts

Picasso marble bear, by Alex Tsethlikai.
Courtesy of Turquoise Village

Rhodacrosite bear, by Abby Quam.
Courtesy of Roxanne and Greg Hofmann

Pipestone bear with turquoise arrowhead and etched flute player, by Gerald Burns.
Courtesy of Turquoise Village

UPPER ROW, *left to right:* Jet mountain lion, by Michael Coble. *Courtesy of Turquoise Village*

Black marble beaver with turquoise and coral arrowhead, by Carlton Etsate.
Courtesy of Turquoise Village

Black marble bear with abalone arrowhead, by Alan Lewis. *Courtesy of Pueblo of Zuni Arts & Crafts*

LOWER ROW, *left to right:* Black marble bird, by Barry Yamutewa. *Courtesy of Turquoise Village*

Black marble lizard with turquoise eyes, by Terry Leonard. *Courtesy of Turquoise Village*

Black marble badger with turquoise eyes, by Todd Etsate. *Courtesy of Turquoise Village*

Jadeite buffalo with turquoise eyes, by Ephran Chavez. *Courtesy of Turquoise Village*

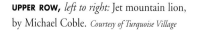

ALL WOOD:

UPPER ROW: Three serpents, by Tiffany Tsabetsaye.

LOWER ROW, *left to right:* Four serpents, by Jones Neha.

Snake with crushed turquoise, by James Delena.

Serpent, by Jones Neha.

Courtesy of Turquoise Village

UPPER ROW, *left to right:* Alabaster horse, by Rodney Laiwakete. *Courtesy of Barbara and Chuck Cooper*

Altar doll of elk antler, by Anderson Weahkee. *Courtesy of Turquoise Village*

CENTER ROW, *left to right:* Alabaster bear with turquoise arrowhead, by Daryl Westika. *Courtesy of Pueblo of Zuni Arts & Crafts*

Black marble bear with turquoise heart-line, by Abby Quam. *Courtesy of Turquoise Village*

LOWER ROW, *left to right:* Pipestone bear with turquoise heart-line, by Abby Quam. *Courtesy of Turquoise Village*

Picasso marble bear with arrowhead of spiny oyster shell and turquoise, by Anderson Weahkee. *Courtesy of Pueblo of Zuni Arts & Crafts*

Alabaster horse, by Hubert Pincion. *Courtesy of Pueblo of Zuni Arts & Crafts*

UPPER ROW, *left to right:* Chinese turquoise bear holding fish made of shell, by Andres Quandelacy. *Courtesy of Turquoise Village*

Two Chinese turquoise bears with silver eyes and heart-line, by Debra Gasper. *Courtesy of Turquoise Village*

Standing bear of Chinese turquoise holding fish made of shell, by Andres Quandelacy. *Courtesy of Roxanne and Greg Hofmann*

Standing bear of Mexican turquoise with jet eyes, by Arnie and Claudia Calavaza. *Courtesy of Turquoise Village*

Chinese turquoise turtle with silver spots, by Debra Gasper. *Courtesy of Turquoise Village*

LOWER ROW, *left to right:* Two Mexican turquoise buffalos, by Rhoda Quam. *Courtesy of Turquoise Village*

Chinese turquoise bear with heart-line, by Andres Quandelacy. *Courtesy of Turquoise Village*

Frog of Sleeping Beauty turquoise with coral eyes, by Clive Hustito. *Courtesy of Pueblo of Zuni Arts & Crafts*

Green turquoise bear, by David Chavez. *Courtesy of Pueblo of Zuni Arts & Crafts*

UPPER ROW, *left to right:* Serpentine eagle, by Estaban Najera. *Courtesy of Pueblo of Zuni Arts & Crafts*

Serpentine bird, by Derrick Kaamasee. *Courtesy of Pueblo of Zuni Arts & Crafts*

SECOND ROW, *left to right:* Serpentine snakes, by Wilfred Cheama. *Courtesy of Pueblo of Zuni Arts & Crafts*

Serpentine lizard, by Vern Nieto. *Courtesy of Turquoise Village*

THIRD ROW, *left to right:* Serpentine lizard, by Anthony Mecale. *Courtesy of Turquoise Village*

Picasso marble lizard, by Terry Leonard. *Courtesy of Turquoise Village*

Picasso marble owl, by Christine Banteah. *Courtesy of Turquoise Village*

LOWER ROW, *left to right:* Serpentine mole, by Fred Weekoty. *Courtesy of Pueblo of Zuni Arts & Crafts*

Picasso marble lizard, by Anthony Mecale. *Courtesy of Pueblo of Zuni Arts & Crafts*

From left to right: Turquoise buffalo with coral horns, by Andres Quandelacy. *Courtesy of Pueblo of Zuni Arts & Crafts*

Coral fox, by Daniel Quam. *Courtesy of Roxanne and Greg Hofmann*

Coral bear with turquoise eyes on a turquoise stand, by Rigney Boone. *Courtesy of Roxanne and Greg Hofmann*

Turquoise bear with jet heart-line, by Andres Quandelacy. *Courtesy of Pueblo of Zuni Arts & Crafts*

Blessing of the Kivas, acrylic, 18 in. x 24 in., by Duane Dishta. At left are two Atoshle (Wright, page 28). The other five, including the two peeping out of the ladder area, are Koyemshi (Wright, pages 40 and 41). From left to right, the Koyemshi are two Posuki, the Pouters; Kalutsi, the Infant, or Suwitsana; Itsepasha, the Glum, or the Captive of the Kianakwe; and Tsathlashi, the Old Youth.

Courtesy of Turquoise Village

Paintings

ZUNI HAS A painting history that is long in duration, but short in the number of artists. The village elders disapproved of painting as an art form, particularly when the subject matter touched on ceremonial behavior. As early as 1918, painting was forbidden in Zuni. In that era Zuni painters would not sign their works, probably to protect themselves from tribal censure.

In the late 1920s Lawasewa painted formal depictions of altars. These paintings were meticulous in detail and rich in colors.

In 1928 and 1929 Patone Cheyatie painted two pictures of rows of Mountain Sheep Dancers. Even though the dancers were more in the tradition of the Rio Grande Pueblos, the paintings were a portent of things to come out of Zuni.

Generally, Zuni work encompassed outlining, both in pencil and color. The delineation was not as meticulous and careful as it was in the paintings of other Pueblo artists.

There were two other Zuni painters whose works merited attention. Teddy Weakee worked in watercolor and oil. His oil painting, *Old Zuni Rock,* was highly esteemed among Indian paintings of the time. Weakee died in 1965.

Percy Sandy, also known as Kai-Sa or Percy Sandy Tsisete, was born in Zuni in 1918. Kai-Sa painted his best work in realistic everyday scenes. He also portrayed dance figures in the Pueblo manner, leaning heavily toward Kachina subjects.

As of the 1960s, the Zuni Pueblo had not developed a school of painting that could be called its own. However, the Kachina paintings of Kai-Sa and the abstracts of Roger Tsabetsaye showed that the talent was there, and that there was a bright future for Zuni paintings.

Today there are many Zuni artists with their own styles. They work in watercolor, acrylic, and oil. The artists tend to favor acrylic because of the quick drying time.

Hubert Patrick Sanchez, born in 1960, is well-known for his kaleidoscopic paintings. His wife, Judy Tsosie, is a jewelry-maker. Patrick, as he prefers to be called, said that in doing this painstaking and meticulous work, he often has to place his hands on the paintings. As a consequence, he uses acrylic that dries quickly.

Patrick has always lived in Zuni except for the three years he was in the National Guard, stationed at Fort Bliss, El Paso, Texas. In 1976, Patrick enrolled for high school painting lessons. His teachers, Mrs. Beam and Mrs. Jean Othole, encouraged him to develop his own style. He realized the sun face design with the rays of the sun emanating in every direction appealed to his spirituality. Patrick feels that life is sacred and wants to transfer that feeling into his paintings.

The kaleidoscopes are his own design. He said that painting the first piece of kaleidoscope is hard, but then the rest of it starts to flow. He tries to keep everything in balance with these paintings and can often work seventeen hours a day, if he is not interrupted. Having four small children in the household makes this an unlikely probability.

Patrick makes miniatures of two inches by three inches so that people who cannot afford his larger paintings may be able to buy the smaller ones. They are so perfectly detailed he has often been asked if he uses a magnifying glass when he paints. He assures everyone that he does not.

James Cachini was born in 1970 in Zuni, and he has always lived in Zuni. When James was nine years old, his sixth grade class went on a field trip to the Old Mission. It was there he saw the painting of Alex Seowtewa. This inspired him to pursue painting. He works only in watercolors. He paints in the old way by outlining in black watercolor, then erasing it and filling in the rest of his painting. James likes to depict Zuni religious life in his paintings, with subjects such as the Corn Mountain or Dowa Yalanne, and the Rain Dancers, who protect earth and moon and keep the world in harmony. He also enjoys doing still life paintings of pottery. He produces approximately fifty twelve-by-sixteen-inch paintings in a month. He sells most of his paintings to local people. James says that he is always thinking of new ideas for painting subjects, that he never seems to run dry.

Phil Hughte was born in Zuni and has lived there except for the four years (1973–1977) he attended Northern Arizona University in Flagstaff, Arizona, where he received his Bachelor of Fine Arts degree.

When Phil was seven years old, he was inspired by the paintings of his wife's uncle, Percy Sandy or Kai-Sa. At the age of seven,

Phil sold his first painting, for one dollar, to C. G. Wallace, who at that time had a trading post in Zuni. Phil paints thirty-five to fifty paintings a year in oils, acrylics, and watercolors. He enjoys painting scenes remembered from his childhood: the landscape, the old buildings, the architecture of the old stone masonry. He focuses his attention on the Zuni people, and he finds the the elders and the young people especially beautiful.

He and his wife, Dru Anne, have a son, Galen, who makes jewelry. Dru Anne makes miniature pottery. Phil teaches art at Zuni High School and enjoys working with the students. He spends most of his summers in Albuquerque, New Mexico, where he works with a master printer. In addition to printmaking he does calligraphy, intaglio, lithography, cartoons, ceramics, and pottery. He has a wonderful sense of humor, seen in his paintings of clowns. He has written a book, *Zuni Artist Looks at Frank Hamilton Cushing,* and illustrated it with his cartoons. In 1995 television station KNME in Albuquerque did a thirty-minute documentary about him.

Duane Dishta was born in Zuni in 1946 and has always lived there. Duane's father, Frankie, is Zuni and his mother, Elizabeth, is three-fourths Zuni and one-fourth Hopi. Duane and his wife, Margie, have relatives in Polacca, Arizona, on the Hopi reservation, where they often attend the Hopi dances.

Duane also takes part in the Zuni ceremonies every year. When there are no ceremonies taking place, he produces approximately four paintings of twenty-four inches by thirty-six inches each month. Duane was originally inspired to paint by the work of two Hopi painters, Ray Naha and Neil David. As a consequence, his paintings always reflect Hopi and Zuni life.

Duane is probably the best-known artist in Zuni. His paintings appeared in Barton Wright's book, *Kachinas of the Zuni,* which depicts 193 Kachinas and other dancers. The paintings, five inches by seven inches, were completed in the 1960s for Nancy and Tom Moore who were teachers at Zuni High School. Duane outlined the figures with colored markers, erased the outlines, and then painted the inside with watercolors. He painted them in the wintertime when there were no ceremonies taking place.

In the 1970s jewelry was so popular that Duane stopped painting and began making jewelry. This lasted until the 1980s, when he returned to his first love, painting. He originally used casein, but he switched to acrylics because he likes the colors and acrylic's fast-drying properties.

Duane has won painting awards at the Gallup Inter-Tribal Indian Ceremonial in Gallup, New Mexico; at the Heard Museum shows in Phoenix, Arizona; and at the American Indian and Western Relic Show in Pasadena, California. Duane was also one of the featured artists in the book *Zuni, the Art and the People,* Volume 2.

In a real sense, the artists of Zuni have truly made an indelible mark in the painting world.

THE FOLLOWING IS AN EXPLANATION OF THE PURPOSE AND FUNCTION OF THE KACHINAS IN THE PAINTINGS.

Ainanuwa or *Mepu* takes care of the Buffalo.

Anahoho whips the boys that are being initiated.

A'thlana is a warrior who kills the Buffalo.

Buffalo Dancer and *Buffalo Maiden* dance in the La'pilawe Dance.

Hehe'a, the Blunderer, is a helper to the Oky'enawe and carries all the material necessary for the grinding of the corn. He is very clumsy.

Hewa Hewa are clowns that dance in a burlesque manner.

Hututu is Saiyatasha's Deputy or Pekwin and reinforces all that the Saiyatasha does.

The *Kianakwes* are not Kachinas, but during their dance they distribute food and commodities to the Zuni.

Kokokshi, the Good or Beautiful Kachina, is a rainmaker.

Kokwele or *Oky'enawe* brings seeds to the houses for planting.

Kolowisi, the Water Serpent, brings corn and seeds for the young boys to plant so that they too will grow. This gives the boys strength.

Koyemshi are the fathers of the Zuni, and no one would deny them whatever was asked, for this would be disastrous. The following are Koyemshi:

> *Eshotsi,* the Bat.
>
> *Itsepasha,* the Glum, or Captive of the Kianakwe.
>
> *Kalutsi,* the Infant or Suwitsana.
>
> *Nalashi,* the Aged One.
>
> *Posuki,* the Pouter.
>
> *Tsathlashi,* the Old Youth.

Kumanshi Domda Caynona is the drummer for the Kumanshi Dance.

Kwelele, along with the Shi-tsukia, brings the New Year to Zuni.

La'pilawe is the Buffalo Dance, also called the Feather String Dance because the Kachinas wear long bands of feathers down their backs.

La'pilawe Okya, the Feather String Girl, is the female counterpart of the La'pilawe.

Mohokwe, the Great Horned Owl, dances in the Mixed Dance and is a hunter and a warrior.

Na'le, the Deer Kachina, brings rain and more deer.

Pautiwa is the Kachina Chief and leader of the village of Kothluwala. He has dignity, kindness, and is beautiful. He shares his wealth with those who are less fortunate.

Saiyatasha, also called Long Horn, brings long life to the Zuni people and orchestrates the Shalako ceremony.

Salimopia Kachinas are runners and also guards of the highest of the Kachinas and of the ceremonies.

The Shalako, the Courier of the Gods, brings corn, seed, and fruit to the Zuni.

Shalako Anuthlona is also called the Shalako Warrior and is the alternate for the Shalako. He helps the Shalako with the heavy mask.

Shi-tsukia, along with Kwelele, brings the New Year to the Zuni.

Shulawitsi Kachinas are the Little Pekwin or Little Fire Gods. They take care of the sun and carry a

juniper bark torch. They are also hunters.

Shulawitsi An Tatchu is the Shulawitsi's ceremonial father. He helps him light his torch and assists him in the planting of the prayer sticks.

Siwilo is the Buffalo and is instrumental in good hunting of all animals.

Tomtsinapa sings with the Laguna Chakwaina Dancers.

Yamuhakto is the Wood Carrier. He is an assistant to Saiyatasha and helps him bring wood to the Zuni.

The following are Hopi Kachinas:

Ang-ak-china, Long-haired Kachina: Their song is to bring rain.

Angwusnasomtaqa or *Tumas,* Crow Mother, carries the yucca sticks that the Hú Kachina uses.

Hú or *Tungwup,* Whipper, whips the boys during their initiation ceremony.

Jemez or *Hemis* distributes the first corn of the year.

Kokopölö or *Kokopelli* or *Hump-backed Flute Player* seduces the girls.

Kokopölö Mana attempts to seduce the men.

Nata-aska, Black Ogre, frightens the children into behaving.

Wuyak-ku-ita, Broad-faced Kachina, is a guard who sees that the Kachinas do not violate their duties.

FROM YEARS PAST:

Untitled, watercolor, 15 in. x 21 in., painted in the late 1960s by Sullivan Shebola. Depicts Shalako, the Courier of the Gods (Wright, page 36), and Koyemshi Tsathlashi, the Old Youth (Wright, page 41). *Courtesy Beverly Vander Wagen Hurlbut*

FROM YEARS PAST:

Untitled, watercolor, 15 in. x 21 in., painted in 1967 by Anthony Edaakie. Depicts Kumanshi Domda Caynona, the Comanche Drummer (Wright, page 121). *Courtesy Beverly Vander Wagen Hurlbut*

FROM YEARS PAST:

Untitled, watercolor, 11½ in. x 18 in., painted in the late 1960s by Sullivan Shebola. Depicts Shulawitsi Kohanna, the Little Pekwin or Little Fire God (Wright, page 109).

Courtesy Beverly Vander Wagen Hurlbut

The Buffalo Dance or La'pilawe Dance, acrylic,
37 in. x 47 in., by Ronnie Cachini. The Kachinas
who perform the Buffalo Dance (Wright, page
120) are, left to right: A'thlana, the Big Stone;
La'pilawe, a variant of La'pilawe, Feather String;
Siwolo, the Buffalo; Ainanuwa or Mepu; and
La'pilawe Okya, the Feather String Girl.
Courtesy of Pueblo of Zuni Arts & Crafts

RIGHT: *Sacred Circle of the Water,* acrylic, 36 in. x 36 in., by Phil Hughte. This painting depicts Kolowisi, the Water Serpent (Wright, page 55). Kolowisi is also known as the Seed Bearer of the Gods. He is the guardian of all underground springs and appears at the initiation of the young boys to bring corn kernels, wheat, pumpkin, and other seeds for the boys to plant. *Courtesy Pueblo of Zuni Arts & Crafts*

OPPOSITE: *The Shalako,* mixed media, 20¼ in. x 24 in., by Alex Seowtewa. Depicts Shalako Kachina, the Courier of the Gods (Wright, page 36).

Courtesy Roxanne and Greg Hofmann

BELOW: *Wrong Directions for the Visiting Clowns and More Clowns,* acrylic, 32 in. x 44 in., by Phil Hughte. The clowns on the left are Anglo clowns, while the others are Hewa Hewa (Wright, page 124).

Courtesy of Pueblo of Zuni Arts & Crafts

Alex Seowtewa '86 ©

OPPOSITE: *Spirits in the Sky,* acrylic, 30 in. x 40 in., by Anthony Sanchez. Depicts Shalako Kachina, the Courier of the Gods, and Koyemshi (Wright, pages 36, 40 and 41).

Private collection

ABOVE: *Blessing for All,* acrylic, 24 in. x 30 in., by Anthony Sanchez. Depicts Saiyatasha, the Rain Priest of the North or Long Horn, and the Hututu, Saiyatasha's Deputy or Pekwin (Wright, page 32).

Courtesy of Turquoise Village

ABOVE: *Shalako,* acrylic, 28 in. x 30 in., by Duane Dishta. Left to right: The Fraternity Altar; Yamuhakto, the Wood Carrier (Wright, page 32); Saiyatasha, the Rain Priest of the North (Wright, page 32); Shalako, the Courier of the Gods (Wright, page 36); Shalako Anuthlona, the alternate for Shalako, also called the Shalako Warrior (Wright, page 36); Koyemshi, Kalutsi, the Infant, or Suwitsana (Wright, page 41); Tsathlashi, the Old Youth (Wright, page 41); Yamuhakto, the Wood Carrier (Wright, page 32); Salimopia Shikan'ona, the Dark Warrior of the Nadir (Wright, page 59); Hututu, Saiyatasha's Deputy or Pekwin (Wright, page 32); and Shulawitsi, the Little Pekwin or Little Fire God (Wright, page 32). *Courtesy of Turquoise Village*

OPPOSITE: *The Dark Warrior of the Nadir,* acrylic, 20 in. x 24 in., by Anthony Sanchez. Depicts Salimopia Shikan'ona, the Dark Warrior of the Nadir (Wright, page 59). *Courtesy of Turquoise Village*

OPPOSITE: *The Coming of the Great Horned Owls,* acrylic, 18 in. x 24 in., by Duane Dishta. Depicts the Mohokwe, the Great Horned Owl Kachinas (Bassman, *Hopi Kachina Dolls and their Carvers,* page 65; Colton, *Hopi Kachina Dolls with a Key to their Identification,* page 78; Wright, *Kachinas: A Hopi Artist's Documentary,* page 111). *Private collection*

ABOVE: *Dance of the Game,* acrylic, 16 in. x 22½ in., by Duane Dishta.

The Kachina coming out of the kiva in the background is Tomtsinapa (Wright, page 103). In front of him is Hehe'a, the Blunderer (Wright, page 109), and in the foreground are four Deer Dancers, Na'le (Wright, page 100).

Courtesy of Pueblo of Zuni Arts & Crafts

Spirits Coming from the Anasazi Ruins, acrylic, 24 in. x 36 in., by Duane Dishta. *Courtesy of Turquoise Village*

The spirits and Kachinas shown in this painting are described below, with references in parentheses to the following books:

Bassman, Theda. *Hopi Kachina Dolls and Their Carvers.* Schiffer Publishing Ltd. West Chester, Pennsylvania, 1991.

Colton, Harold S. *Hopi Kachina Dolls with a Key to their Identification.* University of New Mexico Press. Alburquerque, New Mexico, 1959.

Wright, Barton. *Kachinas of the Zuni.* Northland Press. Flagstaff, Arizona, 1985.

Wright, Barton. *Kachinas: A Hopi Artist's Documentary.* Northland Press and The Heard Museum. Flagstaff, Arizona, 1973.

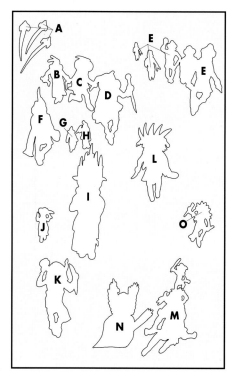

KEY TO IMAGE OPPOSITE:

A—Rainbow Spirits, fifteen in all, in groups of three and six.

B—Anahoho (Wright, *Kachinas of the Zuni*, page 63).

C—Salimopia Shikan'ona, the Dark Warrior of the Nadir (Wright, *Kachinas of the Zuni*, page 59).

D—Salimopia Thluptsin'ona, the Yellow Warrior of the North (Wright, *Kachinas of the Zuni*, page 59).

E—Koyemshi (Wright, *Kachinas of the Zuni*, page 41), from left to right:
Itsepasha, the Glum, or the Captive of the Kianakwe;
Nalashi, the Aged One;
Kalutsi, the Infant, or Suwitsana;
Tsathlashi, the Old Youth;
Eshotsi, the Bat; and
Posuki, the Pouter.

F—Ang-ak-china, Long-haired Kachina, a Hopi Kachina (Bassman, page 81; Colton, #127; Wright, *Kachinas: A Hopi Artist's Documentary*, page 172). Five Long-haired Kachinas are pictured, one large figure and a group of four small ones.

G—Kokopölö Mana or Kokopelmana, Kokopelli Maiden, a Hopi Kachina (Bassman, page 123; Colton, #66; Wright, *Kachinas: A Hopi Artist's Documentary*, page 231).

H—Kokopölö or Kokopelli, Assassin Fly or Robber Fly Kachina or Hump-backed Flute Player Kachina, a Hopi Kachina (Bassman, page 123; Colton, #65; Wright, *Kachinas: A Hopi Artist's Documentary*, page 109).

I—Jemez Kachina, Hemis Kachina, a Hopi Kachina (Bassman, page 106; Colton, #132; Wright, *Kachinas: A Hopi Artist's Documentary*, page 214).

J—Buffalo Maiden.

K—Buffalo Dancer.

L—Nata-aska, Black Ogre, a Hopi Kachina (Bassman, page 128; Colton, #29; Wright, *Kachinas: A Hopi Artist's Documentary*, page 78).

M—Hú Kachina or Tungwup Whipper Kachina, a Hopi Kachina (Colton, #14; Wright, *Kachinas: A Hopi Artist's Documentary*, page 67); two Hú Kachinas are shown.

N—Angwusnasomtaqa or Tumas, Crow Mother, a Hopi Kachina (Bassman, page 99; Colton, #12; Wright, *Kachinas: A Hopi Artist's Documentary*, page 66).

O—Wuyak-ku-ita, Broad-faced Kachina, a Hopi Kachina (Bassman, page 23; Colton, #22; Wright, *Kachinas: A Hopi Artist's Documentary*, page 26); two Broad-faced Kachinas are shown.

Spirit of the Shalako, acrylic, 18 in. x 22 in., by Eldred Sanchez. Depicts the Shalako, the Courier of the Gods, and the Shalako Anuthlona, the alternate for Shalako, also called the Shalako Warrior (Wright, page 36). They are seeking blessings from the rock that once was the Brother and Sister.

Courtesy of Pueblo of Zuni Arts & Crafts

ABOVE: *Shalako Racing,* acrylic, 14 in. x 26 in., by Hubert Patrick Sanchez. This painting features Shalako, the Courier of the Gods (Wright, page 36). The Kachina at bottom left is Salimopia Shelow'ona, the Red Warrior of the South (Wright, page 59). At bottom right is Salimopia Thluptsin'ona, the Yellow Warrior of the North (Wright, page 59). *Courtesy of Pueblo of Zuni Arts & Crafts*

RIGHT: *Three Brave Clown Dancers,* acrylic, 14 in. x 11 in., by Phil Hughte. The dancers are Hewa Hewa (Wright, page 124). *Private collection*

OPPOSITE: *Winter's End Brings New Beginning,* watercolor, 12 in. x 16 in., by James Cachini. Depicts, top right, Shi-tsukia, the White Kachina (Wright, page 19); Pautiwa, the Kachina Chief and the leader of the Kachina village of Kothluwala (Wright, page 15); Kwelele, the Black Kachina (Wright, page 19), who brings the New Year to Zuni; and six Shalakos, the Couriers of the Gods (Wright, page 36). In the third row down are Kokokshi, the Good and Beautiful Kachina, and Kokwele, the Kachina Girl (Wright, page 85). In the bottom row are, left to right: Shulawitsi An Tatchu, Shulawitsi's ceremonial father; Shulawitsi, the Little Pekwin or Little Fire God; Saiyatasha, the Rain Priest of the North or Long Horn; and, behind Long Horn, Yamuhakto, the Wood Carrier (all found in Wright, page 32). *Courtesy of Turquoise Village*

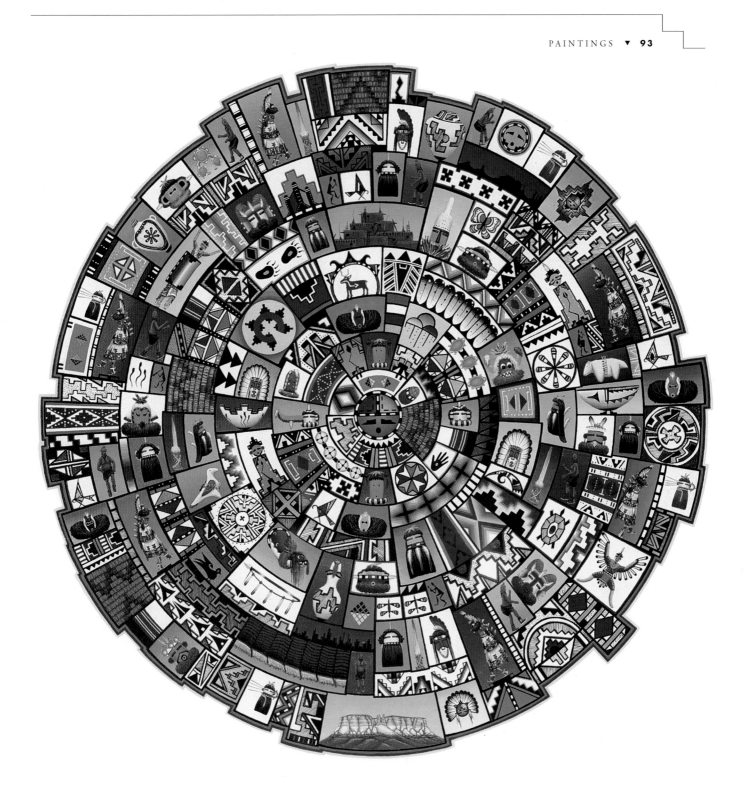

OPPOSITE: *Brother and Sister Rock,* acrylic, 18½ in. x 22¼ in, by Eldred Sanchez. Brother and Sister are holding baskets filled with prayer sticks. During the time of floods, people sought refuge on top of Dowa Yalanne, the Corn Mountain of Zuni. The high priest was to make a human sacrifice of his two children. The children were dressed in their finest clothes and given the baskets. As they stepped into the water it started receding. When the children reached the bottom they were turned into stones, which can be seen until this day. Kolowisi, the Water Serpent (Wright, page 55), made his appearance at the time of the flood.

Courtesy of Pueblo of Zuni Arts & Crafts

ABOVE: *Kaleidoscope,* acrylic, 27 in. x 31½ in., by Hubert Patrick Sanchez. The painting depicts all of the aspects of Zuni life.

Courtesy of Pueblo of Zuni Arts & Crafts

Treasures Unlimited

IN THE ZUNI Pueblo the life of the people is inextricably tied to art and to craft. The majority of Zunis create so that two aims are satisfied. The first is to earn a livelihood; the second, to satisfy an inner need for expression.

Most Zuni artists create jewelry, pottery, fetishes, paintings, beadwork, and Kachinas. These are the major areas of Zuni expertise and interest. However, there are areas that are not so widely known.

In the past, baskets have been important to the Zunis for everyday use and for cere-monial purposes. Through the early 1900s they were made to be used for collecting,

harvesting, and carrying. The baskets made during this period were so heavily used that they are generally not in service any longer.

However, basketmaking was never a craft the Zunis excelled in. We see very few Zuni baskets anywhere, and the baskets in Zuni homes are Apache, Hopi, and Havasupai, usually obtained by trading.

As late as 1931 the Zunis made a plaited yucca basket. The quality was generally coarse, and the basket was decorated with concentric squares. The Zunis also made a plaited ring basket that was used as a pot rest to protect a woman's head from the hot stew bowls that she carried there. The Zunis wove wicker trays and shallow jars with a constricted neck. The trays were shallow, finely woven, undecorated,

Child's swing, made by the Zuni Furniture and Woodworks Enterprise and designed by Marjorie Chavez.
Courtesy Pueblo of Zuni Arts & Crafts

and shallow jars with a constricted neck. The trays were shallow, finely woven, undecorated, and used for sifting fine grain.

Although basketmaking has pretty much disappeared from Zuni life, many new crafts are arising. One of the more exciting new crafts is furniture making. In 1991, the Zuni Furniture and Woodworks Enterprise began operating as a tribal venture. Quentin Peynetsa is the manager, and the business employs seven Zuni craftsmen.

Ponderosa pine is bought in Albuquerque, New Mexico, and brought to the factory in Zuni. The Enterprise makes kitchen cabinets, exterior doors, showcases, curio cabinets, couches, tables, chairs, boxes, screens, upholstery, and children's swings. The woodwork is stained, and very often local artists such as Anthony Sanchez, Edward Lewis, and Hubert Patrick Sanchez paint the items with Zuni designs, symbols, and Kachinas in bold, bright, and beautiful patterns. The furniture enterprise blends design talents with the artistry of Zuni painters.

Painter Duane Dishta has gone a whole new direction with his art. He has begun painting the skins of drums, and a drum painted by him is truly a work of art. On the skin of the drum shown on page 98, Duane painted four Kachina dance elements, depicting the four seasons. On the side of the drum, he painted beautiful Zuni designs. Painting the sides and skin of a drum is the extension of old tribal art painting, when hides, bones, wood, and pottery were the objects of an artist's brush.

Alabaster sculptures are not usually made by the Zunis. It is in fetish carving the Zunis

excel. However, the lizard sculpture and the eagle sculpture on page 99 are very well done. There is much potential for further developement of this medium.

Kolowisi is the Water Serpent whose head protrudes through the altar screen (page 100). His function is to bring water and seeds to the young boys, who will plant these special seeds in an area separate from the regular crop. In addition, the Kachinas dance all night around the altar. Since the altar is prominent in the religion of the Zunis, it is natural for the Kolowisi, the Water Serpent, to make its appearance in heightening the beauty of the ceremony taking place in the kiva.

The Navajos are recognized as prolific weavers, but weaving takes place among the Zunis, too. They make sashes and belts worn in the ceremonial dances, created on upright looms. The women at Zuni do most of the weaving, although men know how to weave and sometimes do. The Zuni loom features the use of a straight stick attached to the warp. This keeps the fabric even throughout its length.

The women produce a white robe embroidered in red, green, and black with a narrow band at the top and a wide one on the lower border. They embroider white kilts of cotton in the same colors as the robes and with raincloud designs.

There is no economic significance in terms of selling these clothes. There is, however, a cultural significance in supplying and making the clothes for ceremonial activities. Today typical American clothes are worn by the Zuni Indians.

Even though the making of Kachina dolls

has been frowned upon by the elders of the Zuni tribe, many Zuni men are carving Kachina dolls and doing fine work. Very few are making miniature dolls, and the collection seen on the page with the finely crafted Shalako House is a good example. The Shalako House is a replica of a typical house in Zuni. The wooden window frames, the exterior masonry, the heavy rounded beams—characteristic of the old Spanish architecture of the Southwest—all add up to wonderful authentic detail.

The art life in the Zuni community is immense. It provides a living for large numbers of Zuni families. The children grow up in this environment with art surrounding them. To learn old art forms is commonplace, and to try new ones is a challenge. The Zunis deservedly have it both ways.

FROM YEARS PAST:

Zuni altar with Kolowisi, the Water Serpent (Wright, page 55). At the back end of the altar is the Hehe'a Kachina, the Blunderer (Wright, pages 72 and 109), early 1900s, artist unknown.

Private collection

FROM YEARS PAST, *left to right:*

Utility basket made of red willow, ca. 1940, artist unknown.

Utility basket made of rabbit brush and edged with bear grass, ca. 1950, artist unknown.

Ring made of yucca, made in 1967 by Fred Davis.

The Zuni name for this ring is Ha:kime. Zuni women used it to protect their heads from the hot stew bowls they carried there.

Courtesy of Dr. T. R. Frisbie

Drum depicting the Four Seasons, 33 in. diameter, painted by Duane Dishta.

SPRING, *top:* Two A'hute (Wright, page 79); Velvet Shirt Dancer; Kokwele, the Kachina Girl (Wright, page 85). The Kachinas are descending into the kiva. These Kachinas bring blessings into the village for the people and the crops.

SUMMER, *right:* Kokokshi, the Good or Beautiful Kachina (Wright, page 85). The Zunis call these the Rain Dancers, who are asking for rains so that the crops may prosper.

AUTUMN, *left:* Pautiwa, the Kachina Chief Leader (Wright, page 15); Shi-tsukia, the White Kachina (Wright, page 19); Kwelele, the Black Kachina (Wright, page 19). These three Kachinas come into the village after a ten-day fasting period to bring in the New Year.

WINTER, *below:* Six Shalako Kachinas, the Couriers of the Gods (Wright, page 36); Three Anuthlona, the alternates for Shalako (Wright, page 36). This Shalako Ceremonial is the year-end celebration of the past year's blessings and offerings.

This drum won First Prize at the Gallup Inter-Tribal Indian Ceremonial in Gallup, New Mexico, in 1990. *Courtesy of Roxanne and Greg Hofmann*

Zuni Pueblo house, by Titus Ukestine.

Sixteen Kachina dolls, approximately 2 in. high, by Darrin Shebola

Courtesy of Milford Nahohai

Alabaster lizard, 11½ in. high, by Terry Leonard.
Courtesy of Judy Johnsen

Alabaster eagle, 9 in. high, by Brian Leonard.
Courtesy of Turquoise Village

Screen, *left,* made by the Zuni Furniture and Woodworks Enterprise and painted by Edward Lewis. The first panel is the Salimopia Itapanahnan'ona, the Many-Colored Warrior of the Zenith (Wright, page 59). The second panel is the Shalako, the Courier of the Gods (Wright, page 36). The third panel is the Salimopia Shikan'ona, the Dark Warrior of the Nadir (Wright, page 59).

Screen, *right,* made by the Zuni Furniture and Woodworks Enterprise and painted by Anthony Sanchez. The first and third panels depict the Kokokshi, the Good or Beautiful Kachina (Wright, page 85). The second panel is the Kokwele, the Oky'enawe or Grinding Maiden (Wright, page 72).

Table and chairs, made by the Zuni Furniture and Woodworks Enterprise and painted by Hubert Patrick Sanchez.

Three boxes, made by the Zuni Furniture and Woodworks Enterprise. Box with dragonflies, *left,* by Marjorie Esalio. Box, center, with Zuni pot design, painted by Hubert Patrick Sanchez. Box, *right,* with rainbird and feathers designed and painted by Marjorie Esalio.

Six dress sashes, by Vivian Kaskalla. These are worn in ceremonial dances.

Blue belt, by Neil Waseta.

Red belt (on chair), by Leander Booqua. This belt won First Place in Fine Arts and Best in Weaving at the Zuni High School Spring Art Show in 1990.

Courtesy of Pueblo of Zuni Arts & Crafts

GLOSSARY

▼▼▼

AMBER A fossilized resin.

BEZEL A sleeve of silver that holds a stone in place.

CHANNEL WORK A style of jewelry-making that uses silver frames in which stones are cut to fit the frame.

CLUSTER WORK A style of jewelry-making that features several small stones, each set in its own bezel.

DEER IN HIS HOUSE A design motif of a deer with a heart-line and surrounded by a white space.

DREMEL A handheld electric tool.

FETISH A stone or shell that is carved to resemble an animal or bird. It is believed to possess a spirit that can give good luck to the owner.

FETISH NECKLACE Miniature carvings of birds or animals strung on heishe necklaces.

HATCHING OR HACHURE The drawing of fine parallel lines on pottery.

HAWIKUH The first Zuni village that came in contact with the Europeans.

HEART-LINE A line leading from the mouth to the torso of an animal, representing the breath of the animal.

HEISHE Hand-rolled stones or shell that have been cut, drilled, and ground into small beads and strung in a necklace.

INLAY The use of stones or shells in a mosaic-like design, enclosed in a bezel.

JET A coal substance.

KACHINA A Kachina is a spirit, and the masked dancers in the ceremonials take on the spirits of the particular Kachinas they portray.

KACHINA DOLL A replica of a Kachina that is sometimes given to the children so that they may learn what the Kachinas look like.

KILN An enclosure for firing pottery.

KIVA A ceremonial chamber.

KNIFEWING (A:CHI'YA'LADABA) A mystical figure.

MATSAYKA The first of Zuni's seven villages.

NEEDLEPOINT A stone that is finished to fine points at each end.

PETIT POINT A stone that is pointed at one end and rounded on the other.

ROSETTE A sacred Zuni medallion.

SHAMAN A priest who uses extraordinary powers for the purpose of curing the sick, divining the hidden, and controlling events.

SLIP A thick solution of clay mixed with water and brushed on a piece of pottery before the designs are painted.

SPIDERWEB TURQUOISE Turquoise with a matrix pattern resembling the web of a spider.

SUN FACE A design showing the face of the sun with its rays emanating in every direction.

TEMPER Sand or finely crushed rock or ground pieces of pottery shards added to the clay in the making of pottery.

SUGGESTED READING

▼▼▼

Bahti, Mark. Pueblo *Stories and Storytellers.* Treasure Chest Publications, Inc. Tucson, Arizona. 1988.

Bahti, Tom. *Southwestern Indian Arts & Crafts.* K. C. Publications. Las Vegas, Nevada. 1966.

———. *Southwestern Indian Tribes.* K. C. Publications. Las Vegas, Nevada. 1968.

Barry, John W. *American Indian Pottery.* Books Americana, Inc. Florence, Alabama. 1981.

Bassman, Theda. *Hopi Kachina Dolls and Their Carvers.* Schiffer Publishing Ltd. West Chester, Pennsylvania. 1991.

Bassman, Theda and Michael. *Zuni Jewelry.* Schiffer Publishing Ltd. West Chester, Pennsylvania. 1992.

Bedinger, Margery. *Indian Silver Navajo and Pueblo Jewelers.* University of New Mexico Press. Alburquerque, New Mexico. 1973.

Bell, Barbara and Ed. *Zuni the Art and the People,* Vol. 1. Squaw Bell Traders. Grants, New Mexico. 1975.

Bennett, Edna Mae and John F. *Turquoise Jewelry.* Turquoise Books. Colorado Springs, Colorado. 1973.

Bunzel, Ruth L. *The Pueblo Potter.* General Publishing Company. Toronto, Ontario, Canada. 1929.

———. *Zuni Katcinas.* The Rio Grande Press. Glorieta, New Mexico. 1929–1930.

Cirillo, Dexter. *Southwestern Indian Jewelry.* Abbeville Press Publishers. New York. 1992.

Cohen, Lee M. *Art of Clay.* Clear Light Publishers. Santa Fe, New Mexico. 1993.

Colton, Harold S. *Hopi Kachina Dolls with a Key to their Identification.* University of New Mexico Press. Albuquerque, New Mexico. 1949.

Cushing, Frank Hamilton. *Zuni Fetishes.* K. C. Publications. Flagstaff, Arizona. 1883.

Eaton, Linda B. *Native American Art of the Southwest.* Publications International. Lincolnwood Illinois. 1993.

Feder, Norman. *American Indian Art.* Harry N. Abrams, Inc. New York. 1965.

Finkelstein, Harold, Dr. *Zuni Fetish Carvings.* South West Connection. Decatur, Georgia. 1994.

Gill, Spencer. *Pottery Treasures.* Graphic Arts Center Publishing Co. Portland, Oregon. 1976.

———. *Turquoise Treasures.* Graphic Arts Center Publishing Co. Portland, Oregon. 1975.

Goddard, Pliny Earle. *Pottery of the Southwestern Indians.* The American Museum of Natural History. New York. 1928.

Harlow, Francis H. *Modern Pueblo Pottery.* Northland Press. Flagstaff, Arizona. 1977.

Harlow, Francis H. and Young, John V. *Contemporary Pueblo Indian Pottery.* Museum of New Mexico Press. Santa Fe, New Mexico. 1965.

Harmsen, Bill. *Patterns and Sources of Zuni Kachinas.* The Harmsen Publishing Company. 1988.

Kirk, Ruth F. *Zuni Fetishism.* Avanyu Publishing, Inc. Albuquerque, New Mexico. 1943.

Levy, Gordon. *Who's Who in Zuni Jewelry.* Western Arts Publishing Co. Denver, Colorado. 1980.

Manley, Ray. *Ray Manley's Portraits & Turquoise of Southwest Indians.* Ray Manely Photography, Inc. Tucson, Arizona. 1975.

———. *Ray Manley's Southwestern Indian Arts & Crafts.* Ray Manely Photography, Inc. Tucson, Arizona. 1975.

McManis, Kent. *A Guide to Zuni Fetishes & Carvings.* Treasure Chest Books. Tucson, Arizona. 1995.

Pike, Donald G. *Anasazi Ancient People of the Rock.* American West Publishing Co. Palo Alto, California. 1974.

Rodee, Marian and Ostler, James. *The Fetish Carvers of Zuni.* The Maxwell Museum of Anthropology of The University of New Mexico. Albuquerque, New Mexico. The

Pueblo of Zuni Arts & Crafts. Zuni, New Mexico. 1990.

Rodee, Marian and Ostler, James. *Zuni Pottery.* Schiffer Publishing Ltd. West Chester, Pennsylvania. 1986.

Tanner, Clara Lee. *Indian Baskets of the Southwest.* University of Arizona Press. Tucson, Arizona. 1983.

———. *Southwest Indian Craft Arts.* University of Arizona Press. Tucson, Arizona. 1968.

———. *Southwest Indian Painting.* University of Arizona Press. Tucson, Arizona. 1957.

Toulouse, Betty. *Pueblo Pottery of the New Mexico Indians.* Museum of New Mexico Press. Santa Fe, New Mexico. 1977.

Trimble, Stephen. *Talking with the Clay.* School of American Research. Santa Fe, New Mexico. 1987.

Turnbaugh, William A. and Turnbaugh, Sarah Peabody. *Indian Jewelry of the American Southwest.* Schiffer Publishing, Ltd. West Chester, Pennsylvania. 1988.

Webb, William and Weinstein, Robert A. *Dwellers at the Source.* Grossman Publishers. New York. 1973.

Wormington, H. M. and Neal, Arminta. *The Story of Pueblo Pottery.* Denver Museum of Natural History. Denver, Colorado. 1951.

Wright, Barton. *Kachinas: A Hopi Artist's Documentary.* Northland Publishing. Flagstaff, Arizona. 1973.

———. *Kachinas of the Zuni.* Northland Press. Flagstaff, Arizona. 1985.

INDEX OF ARTISTS

▼▼▼

GENERAL INDEX

▼▼▼

ABOUT THE AUTHOR

THEDA BASSMAN was led by back-packing and river-running exploits into Arizona and New Mexico, where she was pleased to find that her feelings for nature and the environment were rather similar to those expressed by many Native Americans of the region. She developed many friendships within the Native American communities in a short period of time. For the past fifty years she has traveled to Indian lands in the Southwest, not only to visit her friends but to buy their crafts. In 1972 she opened a gallery in Beverly Hills, California, called The Indian and I. When she and her husband retired, they moved to Palm Desert, California, where they now live. They also have a cabin on the Mogollon Rim in northern Arizona, where they spend their time in the forest and traveling to the nearby Indian reservations. Theda has judged Indian shows at the Museum of Northern Arizona in Flagstaff, Arizona; the Gallup Inter-Tribal Indian Ceremonial in Gallup, New Mexico; the Santa Fe Indian Market in Santa Fe, New Mexico; the O'Odham Tash in Casa Grande, Arizona; and the American Indian and Western Relic Show in Pasadena, California. Theda Bassman is a feminist, an environment-alist, and a lover of chamber music. She is a member of Greenpeace, the Sierra Club, and the Hemlock Society, and is a Hospice volunteer.

ABOUT THE PHOTOGRAPHER

Chris Everett

GENE BALZER is a professor of photo-graphy at Northern Arizona University in Flagstaff. He has photographed most of the collection of the Museum of Northern Arizona, also in Flagstaff, and conducts field trips to various archaeological sites and national parks on the Colorado Plateau. Balzer's photographs have appeared in *Arizona Highways, American Indian Art Magazine, Southwest Profile, Plateau* magazine, *The World and I,* and *The Indian Country Guide.* One of his photographs was featured on the cover of a compact disc by Native American flutist R. Carlos Nakai. Balzer is the photo-grapher for all of Theda Bassman's books.